FabJob Guide

Become a Spa Owner

JEREMY MCCARTHY AND JENNIFER JAMES

FABJOB GUIDE TO BECOME A SPA OWNER
by Jeremy McCarthy and Jennifer James

ISBN 978-1-894638-83-8

Library and Archives Canada Cataloguing in Publication

McCarthy, Jeremy
FabJob guide to become a spa owner / Jeremy McCarthy and
Jennifer James.

Includes bibliographical references.
ISBN 978-1-894638-83-8

1. Health resorts--Management. I. James, Jennifer II. Title.
III. Title: Become a spa owner.

RA794.M32 2005   646.7'2'068   C2005-904843-3

Important Disclaimer: Although every effort has been made to ensure this guide is free from errors, this publication is sold with the understanding that the authors, editors, and publisher are not responsible for the results of any action taken on the basis of information in this work, nor for any errors or omissions. The publishers, and the authors and editors, expressly disclaim all and any liability to any person, whether a purchaser of this publication or not, in respect of anything and of the consequences of anything done or omitted to be done by any such person in reliance, whether whole or partial, upon the whole or any part of the contents of this publication. If expert advice is required, services of a competent professional person should be sought.

About the Websites Mentioned in this Guide: Although we aim to provide the information you need within the guide, we have also included a number of websites because readers have told us they appreciate knowing about sources of additional information. (**TIP:** Don't include a period at the end of a web address when you type it into your browser.) Due to the constant development of the Internet, websites can change. Any websites mentioned in this guide are included for the convenience of readers only. We are not responsible for the content of any sites except FabJob.com.

FabJob Inc.   FabJob Inc.
19 Horizon View Court   4616 25th Avenue NE, #224
Calgary, Alberta, Canada T3Z 3M5   Seattle, Washington, USA 98105

To order books in bulk phone 403-949-2039
To arrange a media interview phone 403-949-4980

www.FabJob.com

Contents

About the Authors

Lead author **Jeremy McCarthy** is the spa director at the La Costa Resort and Spa. Prior to his work with La Costa, Jeremy worked for Four Seasons Hotels and Resorts for 14 years, including a major renovation of the Four Seasons Resort in Maui, which was named the number-three resort spa in  the world by *Condé Nast Traveler* magazine. His experience with Four Seasons allowed Jeremy to visit and learn from some of the greatest spa properties in the world, including the Biltmore Hotel in Santa Barbara, Four Seasons Los Angeles, the Regent Beverly Wilshire in Beverly Hills, Four Seasons Las Vegas, Four Seasons Cairo at First Residence, and Four Seasons Resort Punta Mita near Puerto Vallarta, Mexico.

 Editor and contributing author **Jennifer James** leads the editorial department at FabJob Inc., the world's leading publisher of information about dream careers. She has edited, researched for, and contributed to more than 30 FabJob career guides, including *FabJob Guide to Become a Fashion Designer* and *FabJob Guide to Become a Makeup Artist*, as well as Amazon.com bestseller *Dream Careers* by Tag and Catherine Goulet. She also consults one-on-one with entrepreneurs to help them with business development issues.

 **Kibibi Springs** is the owner/creative partner of Moodivations, a total wellness company specializing in mobile spa services and home spa products. In her 10 years as a PR specialist for the beauty industry, Kibibi created and executed successful public relations campaigns for Merle Norman Cosmetics, The Milken Foundation and Sebastian International, as well as Internet and business development strategies for The Wella Corporation and its customer base of salons and spas. In addition, Kibibi is a freelance communications consultant under the moniker Springboard Communications, dedicated to projects that positively affect our mental states, physical capabilities and emotions. She is a UC Santa Barbara alumna, with a B.A. in Communications.

Todra Payne is a freelance writer and seminar speaker with 10 years' experience in the beauty and wellness industries. Companies such as Bath & Body Works and DKNY have used her expertise for product launches and employee image consulting. Also a former professional makeup artist, her artistry has been featured in national and international fashion and lifestyle magazines such as *Elle, Harper's Bazaar, O, Redbook, Martha Stewart's Living* and *W*, as well as on designer's runways and television. She is also a self-proclaimed spa junkie. She can be reached at todrapayne@att.net.

 **Mary Phillips Gintoli** began her beauty industry career more than 15 years ago in New York City as an editor for *Mademoiselle* magazine. She then spent nine years working for two major beauty industry corporations as an advertising copywriter, penning award-winning package copy and ads that have appeared in national women's magazines. She has also worked as a journalist and contributing editor for a variety of newspapers, reporting on fashion and beauty trends. Mary graduated from Sacred Heart University in Connecticut with a B.A. in English and Journalism. Currently a freelance writer and editor, she lives in southern Connecticut with her husband, Joseph, and their two beautiful daughters, Cristina and Alexandra.

Acknowledgments

This book could not have been written without the help of the following experts in the spa industry, who stepped forward to share their secrets for success with you:

- Susanne Bracken
  Calgary, Alberta

- Ann Brown, Spa Director
  Spa Shiki at The Lodge of Four Seasons

- Kristin Chou, Director of Service
  Stonewater — A Collection of Spas

- Angela Courtwright, Owner
  Spa Gregorie's
  www.spagregories.com

- Norma Daniel
  HighFields Country Inn and Spa
  www.highfields.com

- Stacey Denney, Founder & Owner
  Barefoot & Pregnant

- Neil Ducoff
  Strategies Publishing Group Inc.
  www.strategies.com

- Ron Folkman, President/CEO
  Specialty Search International Inc.

- Alison Howland
  Director of Global Spa Development, Aveda

- Lori Hutchinson, Owner
  Hutchinson Consulting
  www.hutchinsonconsulting.com

- John Korpi
  SpaQuest International

- Joan Komorowski, CEO
  Joan PR & Marketing

- Jamie Lewis
  Glacier House Resort and Alpine Meadows Spa
  www.glacierhouse.com

- Terri L. Malueg-Ray, Founder and President
  Royal Paws Resort & Day Spa

- Christian Mayr and Stephen J. Renard
  Renard International Hospitality Search Consultants
  www.renardinternational.com

- Ben McConnell
  Word of Mouth Marketing Expert
  co-author of *Creating Customer Evangelists*

- Lynne McNees, President
  International Spa Association
  www.experienceispa.com

- Larry W. Miller Jr., Esq.
  Miller Law Group, PLLC

- Krista Mingo, Spa Founder, Owner and CEO
  Simply Body Day Spa
  Shelton, Connecticut, USA

- Vivienne O'Keeffe
  Vivienne O'Keeffe & Associates Inc.
  www.spaprofits.com

- Stephanie Palko, Founder and Owner
  Copperfalls Aveda Day Spa

- Melanie Schmidt
  Spa Payot

- Sylvia Sepielli, Owner
  Sylvia Planning and Design

- Alexis Ufland, President
  Lexi Design
  www.lexidesign.com

- John Uhrig, President & CEO
  Monochrome Marketing Solutions, Inc.
  www.spamarketing.ca

- Julie Wilson, Editor, *Pulse Magazine*
  International Spa Association

- Leslie Wolski
  Spa Operations and Management Consultant

1. Introduction

Welcome to the exciting world of spa ownership! Opening a new business is one of the most challenging and exciting things that you will ever experience. You are moving into a phase of total freedom in your life — no more punching a clock, designated break times or miserable bosses for you.

As spa owner, you make the decisions, and you grow your business in the direction you choose. You will experience the pure reward of promoting a healthy lifestyle for others. Being satisfied and successful by helping other people to have more happiness, health, and well-being is what owning and operating a spa is all about.

The salary level or profit margin for the spa owner has no limits. Small day spa owners may take home $80,000 to $100,000 or more, depending on the size of the spa, the location and the clientele. Owners of larger resort-style spas may take home considerably more than $100,000.

If a healthy, active and relaxed lifestyle appeals to you, then this is a great environment to spend most of your time. As a spa owner, partaking of spa services on a regular basis is a mandatory part of the job. You will need to test out new services, evaluate staff members, as well as check out the competition. This means getting regular massages, facials, and body treatments whenever possible. Can you handle that?

Of course, there are some risks to this venture, which is why the *FabJob Guide to Become a Spa Owner* exists. This book is designed to help you plan for, open, and operate a fabulously successful spa of your own. The more prepared you are, the more likely you are to hit the ground running when you jump into this burgeoning industry.

1.1   What is a Spa?

The word spa probably comes from the name of the town, Spa, in Belgium famous for over 600 years for its healing hot springs. Some say it is an acronym for the Latin phrase, "Sanus (or Salus) Per Aqua", meaning "health by water." The concept of healing baths and waters is widely considered to have sprung forth from the Greek and Roman cultures, but really, virtually every civilization has used waters for healing in one form or another.

We have all heard the word "spa" used to describe a simple whirlpool tub or a steam room, but it is also used to define facilities that offer specific health, wellness and beauty services such as:

- Massages

- Facials and skin treatment

- Full body treatments, like scrubs or wraps

- Hydrotherapy (water treatments)

- Manicures and pedicures

- Hair cut, color and styling

- Nail treatments

- Makeup application

- Wellness consultation

Trained massage therapists, estheticians, nail technicians, makeup artists, or in some cases other professionals such as nurses or dieticians perform these services for clients in a private or semi-private setting. Clients may purchase a single service, or a package of spa services for their visit.

The spa atmosphere is generally clean, simple, and relaxing. Sounds of nature or relaxation music are often playing in the background, lighting is usually dimmed and natural as possible, and clients are offered simple robes and towels to wear or rest on while they receive their spa treatment.

Clients can stay at the spa for anywhere from an hour to several days. Spas that complete their services in a few hours (for a simple facial or massage) or a single day are known as day spas, while spas that operate in conjunction with stay-over or hotel facilities are known as destination or resort spas. There is also a growing trend towards offering mobile spa services, where spa services are offered to clients in their own home or office.

1.2   The Spa Market

If you ask anyone who owns a spa, they will tell you that this business is much more than just a job — it is a way of life. In fact, "spa industry" does not fully capture what this business has become. The words culture, lifestyle, and spa movement better indicate the important place that spas now hold in our society.

In a recent International Spa Association (ISPA) survey of spa-goers, spa treatments were a top choice for spending $200 of discretionary income, coming in ahead of shopping, the movies, music concerts, and even other beauty treatments.

Confirming the strong hold that the spa business has taken in the hearts and minds of the American public, there were approximately 110 million spa visits made in the U.S. in 2003, and that year the U.S. spa industry generated an estimated $9.4 billion in revenues, according to the ISPA.

The ISPA estimated the number of spas in the U.S. to be almost 15,000 in 2007, representing a 48 percent increase since 2003. More and more people are now recognizing spa visits as an important part of their lives.

The spa business is continuing to flourish despite weak economic conditions, war, terrorism and a whole slew of other factors that have hurt every other sector of the hospitality industry. In a way, though, it makes sense — the more stress and anxiety that exist in our culture, the more people feel a need for relief and comfort.

You should also know that you don't need to live in a big city to operate a successful spa. In addition to local clientele, many small towns are actually more attractive for urban spa-goers since it gives them a chance to get out of the city and relax. For example, the little prairie town of Moose Jaw in Canada (population 34,000) has become well-known as an international spa destination, due partially to its naturally mineral-rich water.

1.3 Benefits of the Career

Running a spa is a job where you will see the results of your hard work on a daily basis, reflected in the faces and body language of satisfied clients. You will be the gracious host for your guests, planning for, creating and maintaining the most comfortable environment to help them relax and enjoy their visit. Here are some of the benefits of this fabulous career choice.

Help People Feel Good

Spas serve the main purpose of helping clients feel better on their way out than they did on their way in. In some ways, your job will be like a doctor, nurse, or counselor. You and your spa will bring relaxation, increased self-confidence, and overall health and wellness to your clients. You will enrich people's lives by offering them a chance to heal themselves physically and mentally.

Spa owners are usually in this business because they like to make other people feel better, and are looking for more meaning in their professional life. A career in spas is full of meaning as you get to touch people's lives in such a positive way. People come to the spa to feel good and get back in touch with what is important to them.

Unlimited Spa Services

To most people, "a day at the spa" is an extravagance that they don't treat themselves to nearly enough. When you own a spa, the spa atmosphere is just another day at the office. Even if you don't take advantage of your spa's services daily, you can't really ask for a more relaxing work environment.

If you need to slip away for a bit of relaxation after a tough day, everything will be at your fingertips, and your employees will be available for consultation on the latest in health and wellness. You will also be in the enviable position of having spa services available to give away to friends, family, and business associates. Just imagine all the new friends you'll find yourself with.

Be Your Own Boss

As the owner of your spa you will have total control over the decisions that are made and the way your spa is run. You will see your dreams and ideas become reality. You will be the creative mind behind the business, and constantly be looking for new ways to spice up your business with new treatments or products.

One of the best parts of this industry is being able to express yourself creatively and establishing what is different about you and your spa from any other spas out there.

Unlimited Profit Potential

When you own a business, you reap the financial rewards of your hard work. When your spa business is up and running, a profit margin in the six-figure range is certainly within the realm of possibility.

In fact, according to data released in 2004 by the ISPA, the average per-spa annual revenue of their member spas is $2.5 million, and $655,000 for non-members. They reported a per-spa profit margin among their member spas of 16%, and for their non-members, 8%. According to a study on the Canadian spa industry conducted at Cornell University, industry revenues reached $1.5 billion nationwide in 2003, up a whopping 146% from two years earlier.

Opening more than one spa can be even more lucrative. Franchising or licensing your spa concept is yet another option to grow your business and make even more of a profit.

A Place in Your Community

As a spa owner you will get to know a lot of people. It is a very social business, and with knowing all these people comes lots of invitations to special events, private parties, charity auctions, and anything else of a social nature. If you are social and like to be involved in your community, you will find many doors are opened to you.

This is because you will not only get on a first-name basis with your everyday customers, but with the customers who have discretionary income and an interest in looking and feeling their best: actors and models, politicians, the morning news anchor, and so on. When they are in your spa, you are the one they want to talk to.

1.4 Inside This Guide

This guide is designed to take you step by step through planning for, developing, opening and running your own spa. Following this Introduction is Chapter 2 (*"Spa Basics"*), which leads you into the world of spa ownership. You'll learn about the spa environment and where you'll fit in as owner, the types of treatments you can offer to your clients, and ways to specialize. You'll also find a section on how to get yourself ready for this big adventure.

Chapter 3 (*"Planning Your Spa"*) is going to help you take all those ideas in your head and get them down on paper. You'll start with some brainstorming and market research, and then review your business options. You'll then get instructions on how to write and refine your spa's business plan, as well as calculate your start-up costs and look for financing if necessary.

Chapter 4 is all about *"Preparing to Open,"* from choosing the right location for your type of spa, to working with engineers and contractors, to decorating. You'll get a list of the equipment and supplies you'll need to perform spa services, as well as who you will need to hire to work in your spa. You'll also get valuable guidance on designing your menu of services, and the licenses you'll need to open your business.

Chapter 5 (*"Running Your Spa"*) is your manual for success and profitability. You will discover how to work out systems for the day-to-day operations such as booking appointments, selling retail products, managing and motivating your employees, accommodating groups of guests, handling complaints, and evaluating your financial performance.

Chapter 6 (*"Getting Clients"*) explains how you attract and keep the lifeblood of your spa business: your clients. You'll read about conventional and unconventional ways to stir interest in your spa, the promotional tools you'll use, and most importantly, how to get clients to become "customers for life".

The guide contains helpful checklists you can use to start and run your spa, sample budgets, sample excerpts of an actual spa business plan, and more. The Conclusion at the end of the guide offers a list of online resources with websites of suppliers, professional associations, and sources of more information.

Now if you are ready, it's time to take the first step. You could be opening the doors to your brand new spa in a very short time from now!

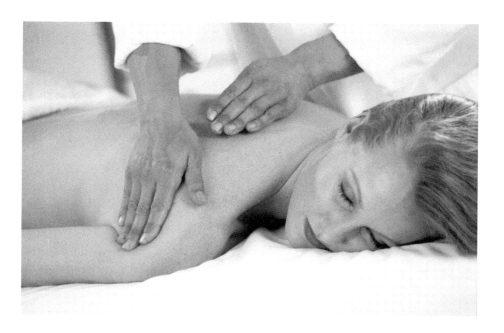

2. Spa Basics

If you're going to run a spa, you'll want to learn as much as possible about how a spa operates. If you've only been to the spa a time or two, there will be plenty to absorb in this chapter, and even if you are an admitted spa "junkie," read on — the spa world changes fast, and there may be new types of specialties and treatments you have yet to discover.

2.1 The Spa Environment

While you certainly can't say that all spas are the same, in general they have basic elements that clients expect:

- Customer calls or comes in to schedule an appointment

- Customer arrives for his or her appointment and enjoys the selected service

- Customer "checks out" after enjoying their service

That's it! These three things pretty much sum up about 95% of a normal day in the operation of the spa. Here is a look at the typical spa environment, as well as some ideas on how to stand out with something unique.

2.1.1   Types of Spas

The type of spa you will open will be based on factors such as personal preference, your background and interests, the start-up capital you have available, the space you have available (if you have a location in mind) and what your market research or gut instinct says is needed in your area.

You don't need to decide on a type of spa right away, so take some time to learn a bit about your options early on in the game. In general, most spas can be classified into one of the following types.

Day Spa

The day spa has shown considerable popularity and growth due to today's fast-paced lifestyle. People don't always have a weekend or even a full day to devote to pampering themselves, so a spa that offers select services that can be completed in an hour or two can be a great niche to explore.

Day spas also have a reputation of offering a less costly spa experience than resort or destination spas, and so may be more attractive to people in the middle-to-upper income ranges.

Day spas usually offer a basic menu of body treatments, massage, facial, and nail care services. Some day spas offer the addition of makeup application and signature facial and body treatments, and may include a light snack or lunch as part of their amenities. Clients can usually opt for individual treatments, half-day or full-day packages.

Services are provided on a daily basis so men and women can come to relax, unwind, and be pampered, if only for an hour or two. They generally do not offer fitness classes or overnight stays like a destination spa might.

Day spas may be completely independent, or they may be what is generally referred to as a "concept spa", which is a spa that is affiliated with and promotes a particular kind of cosmetic products. More information about day spas is available from the Day Spa Association at **www.dayspaassociation.com**.

Salon Spa

Salon spas generally come about through a partnership between a salon owner and a spa owner, or an expansion of an existing salon to incorporate spa services. In fact it has become popular for salons to expand to include day spa services, becoming salon/day spa combos.

This arrangement combines all the amenities and treatments provided by a full service hair care salon (hair styling, cut, color and perming services) as well as certain (usually more simple) spa services.

Clients appreciate the one-stop shop approach, and tend to visit more frequently since they are coming for hair or beauty services that are necessary with greater frequency — hair cutting, waxing, or root touch-ups can't be put off as easily as a massage!

The salon spa usually features one separate area set apart to administer spa services in a calm, quiet atmosphere, and another area set apart for hair care services, where the noise of the blow-dryers and general chatter will not disturb spa patrons.

Mobile or Home Spas

Mobile spas do onsite spa services at special events, parties, and team-building exercises, or just treat a couple of friends to a fabulous pampering spa experience in the comfort of their own home, office, or hotel room.

How you offer the mobile spa experience is limited only by your imagination. A 2004 article in the *Wall Street Journal* detailed some of the unique approaches of a mobile spa franchise company called MobileSpa, including setting up the room with relaxing fountains, candles and music in advance. "The 10 guests chatted, sipped Chardonnay, soaked their feet, and had their nails manicured," described author Kemi Osukoya in the article.

The concept is catching on fast, and is a hot opportunity. Spa goers are tending to like the idea of have a "social" spa experience with friends, and of course, not having to leave their home. Spa professionals like that they don't need to finance the purchase of or pay expensive rent on a brick-and-mortar facility.

Hotel or Hospitality Spas

These spas exist as one part of a larger hospitality service, and are generally just one amenity that the facility offers. In addition to within hotels, hospitality spas can be found at many bed and breakfast inns, casinos, private clubs, fitness centers, and even on cruise ships.

Hotel spas tend to be more "pampering" than day spas, catering to high-end clientele who are traveling or vacationing and want to keep up with their wellness routine, or are looking for a way to relax. The hotel spa may operate as a day spa as well, offering services and facilities to local community members. They offer a typical spa menu, generally centering on facial and body treatments, nail care, massage and water therapies administered by trained spa professionals.

This is a growing market since hotel-goers have come to expect the little extras. While opening a hotel or resort is beyond the scope of this guide, there is the possibility of partnering with a hospitality or tourism service, and setting up your spa within their facility as a business of its own.

Hotels owners are busy running their hotels, and may be grateful to find a reasonably simple answer to offering an additional amenity. This partnership becomes an easier sell the longer your spa has been in business, since you'll have your expertise to offer, as well as your spa's good name.

Medical or Health Spas

Medical spas represent a small but growing percentage of the spa market. Patrons frequent the medical spa for such services as cosmetic dental treatments, microdermabrasion techniques, chemical skin peels, Restylane and Botox injections, laser hair removal and photo facial procedures.

The medical spa is supervised by a licensed and practicing physician, so if this is not you, it will be your partner or director. In addition, staff generally includes nurses, licensed dermatologists and sometimes dentists who perform a variety of procedures.

The medical spa atmosphere tends to be less "pampering" and more "clinical" since they are directly trying to help their customers improve their health. This spa may also provide standard spa services for face and body treatments and post-procedure treatments, as well as a physical therapy clinic or a wellness facility. Other programs available center on weight loss, detoxing, and even psychological counseling services. You can find more information about medical spas from the International Medical Spa Association at **www.medicalspaassociation. org**.

A similar set-up is found in a holistic health center, which offers spa and other services to treat specific ailments and help their customers improve their health by using alternative medicine. In addition to spa services they may offer meditation and breathing classes, tai chi, acupuncture, herbal remedies, and even palm reading.

Because they offer medical or paramedical services, medical spas are subject to a number of the same legal and licensing requirements as other health care providers. One that you must be aware of as owner is HIPAA, or the Health Insurance Portability and Accountability Act, which dictates important regulations regarding the privacy of medical records. You can find out more at **www.experienceispa.com/ISPA/ Education/Resources/HIPAA.htm**.

Destination Spas

A destination spa is different from a hotel or resort spa in that it is not a "bonus service", but is the main attraction. It incorporates the spa experience with a health-oriented, total-wellness vacation. Through personalized fitness, wellness, and health and diet programs guests learn the importance of adopting and maintaining a healthy lifestyle. They can opt for a weekend getaway, a weeklong vacation or more.

In addition to offering traditional and specialty spa services, the destination spa most likely includes hotel and restaurant services, fitness classes, group excursions, and physical activities such as yoga and tai chi. Seminars and lectures on various topics, such as health issues, cooking and nutrition may also be offered.

Professionals on staff include hotel executives, restaurant managers and chefs, dieticians, trained spa personnel, retail sales staff, fitness experts, and medical experts and may even include a visiting physician or staff physician.

In addition to learning about spa services, destination spa owners require knowledge in restaurant management, fitness training, nutrition planning, and hotel management. If you are considering opening a destination spa, you will likely want to partner with friends, family or business associates to help you offer this wide range of hospitality services, while you focus on the spa programming.

2.1.2   Spa Staff Members

Here is an overview of typical spa personnel, their duties and salary ranges. Keep in mind that training, duties and salary levels may vary from spa to spa, state to state, and region or province.

Director

As owner it is up to you whether or not you hire a spa director, since many of the director's duties will overlap with yours. If you are planning on removing yourself from the day-to-day operations then a director or manager will be necessary, but you want to look at your bottom line when you are making this decision.

Remember, the director's salary will be coming straight out of your profits. Most new day spa owners cut their costs when they are just starting out by filling this role themselves, at least until they grow the spa to a bigger size.

If you opt to hire a spa director right away, his or her skill set should balance any areas you are weaker in. They may have a few years of experience in the spa or hospitality field, or a business or related degree from a college or university. Their responsibilities would include overseeing the day-to-day operations of the spa, hiring and firing employees, maintaining good relationships with clients, marketing, communications and public relations duties, and working with sales representatives.

TIP: If you are not experienced in setting up or running spas (and most people aren't) you might consider hiring your spa director on contract while you are in the planning stages of setting up your spa. He or she will be familiar enough with the business to advise you, and will likely charge less than a professional consultant.

Manager or Assistant Director

A manager or assistant director is particularly handy if your spa is open more hours than you or your director can be there, or if you have a large number of staff who have to be scheduled and managed. You would look for someone with a college business degree or sufficient experience in the spa, beauty or hospitality industry and possibly in the area of management.

Duties include assisting the director or owner in the day-to-day operations of the spa, maintaining the cleanliness of the spa, organizing the employees' schedules, maintaining computer files, keeping inventories and ordering supplies, sales and administration and interacting with clients.

Receptionist

The spa receptionist must be well groomed, have great people and communication skills, and be willing to answer phones, greet clients, book appointments, and keep files or computer records.

Sales experience can be a real help in this role. It's important to use care when you hire your receptionist, as he or she will be a deciding factor for many clients on whether to book your services or return for another visit. If someone is not happy with the service they received at your spa, it's just as likely something that happened in the booking, waiting or paying for services, not necessarily in your treatment rooms.

One spa director interviewed for this guide told us he recently hired a spa receptionist who had been working at a veterinary clinic, because her experience was exactly what was needed: "Someone who could book appointments, check guests in, collect payment, work administratively, and handle difficult customers. Granted, her difficult customers were Jack Russell Terriers who were not potty-trained, but you would be surprised at how strong a correlation that can be!"

Massage Therapists

A certified massage therapist will generally have 9 to 18 months of training at a recognized institute. Some spas require prior experience in the field before hiring this spa professional. Refresher courses on the newest and latest techniques will enhance this professional's experience level and marketability to spa clients.

The therapist must have good interpersonal relationships and is generally responsible for performing a variety of massage techniques, for consulting with the client on massage preferences, and for maintaining a calm, quiet atmosphere for the client.

More information about massage therapists is available from the American Massage Therapy Association at **www.amtamassage.org** and Associated Bodywork and Massage Professionals at **www.abmp.com**.

Salon Spa Professionals

The esthetician must be versed in all areas of skin care and waxing services and would possibly be required to have some experience before working at a spa. He or she must have great communication and people skills, be able to analyze a client's skin type or skin care problems and be able to advise client on skin care regime and follow-up treatments. He or she must be impeccably groomed and be able to maintain a serene environment for the client. She may also be asked to sell skin care products.

The nail technician must have a good command of nail care procedures, and be able to identify any nail problems the client may have. The nail technician must perform manicures and pedicures properly without hurting or harming the client and must maintain all his or her equipment. She or he may also be required to sell nail care products.

The same holds true for the hair care professional, who should have experience in cutting and styling, and training in perming and color treatments, and know how to decide the right products for use on a client's hair. He or she must also have great communication skills in order to interpret clients' wishes, and may be required to sell hair care products as well.

In most regions, certification for these positions usually requires a minimum of 250 hours of training at a recognized institute of esthetics or cosmetology. Your state board of cosmetology or professional licensure will be able to advise you on up-to-date regulations in your region. The International Spa Association maintains a list of contact information for each state on its website at **www.experienceispa.com/ISPA/Education/Resources/Cosmetology+Boards.htm**.

A spa technician is a general term used to refer to anyone who works in a spa, but it can also be used to refer to a spa employee who is not licensed to performed cosmetology, esthetician or massage services. This employee can lead clients to their treatment rooms, do laundry, turn on baths, check on clients, and clean rooms after treatments. You might also hire a housekeeper or cleaning service instead.

Medical Spa Professionals

At a medical spa, in addition to traditional spa personnel and massage therapists, you will also find licensed physicians, dermatologists, dentists, nutritionists and registered nurses.

Physicians, dermatologists, and dentists are required to complete a 4-year undergraduate college or university degree, a 3 or 4-year medical school degree program, a 1 to 3-year residency or internship program, and pass a licensing exam to receive a license to practice. Their duties center on all aspects of the patient's or guest's physical health, including consulting with patients or guests, reviewing medical charts and prescribing treatment.

The registered nurse must complete a 2 to 3 year training course in nursing and pass a licensing exam. Some facilities may require their nursing staff to take extra hours of training to be certified in specific procedures, such as laser hair removal services.

The nutritionist must complete a four-year college or university undergraduate degree and possibly one year or more of an internship at a position within the nutritional field. He or she will consult with patients or guests on their eating habits, prescribe their nutritional and supplemental needs, suggest a sensible meal plan for the patient's individual needs and tastes, and monitor patients' progress.

A Day in the Life of a Spa Director

One of the contributing authors of this guide, spa director Jeremy McCarthy, provides the following insight into his typical day running a spa. See if you can picture yourself having a day like this....

7:30 a.m.   I arrive early to walk through the spa and inspect for cleanliness. I notice some dust and make a note to contact our night cleaners; I also see that a light bulb is out. In the spa lounge, I fluff the pillows and neatly arrange the magazines. I head back to my office to check emails and voicemail, as well as peruse the latest financial reports so I can quickly review how we are doing on our month-to-date revenue compared to our budget.

8:00 a.m.   I greet the staff for that morning to be sure everyone is ready for the day. One of our therapists left a voicemail message that she was not feeling well and would stay home. I ask the receptionist to move her appointments to other therapists and let me know if we need to call anyone else in to cover. At the front desk, I quickly review the day and also point out to the staff a couple of V.I.P. guests who are checking into the spa for appointments that afternoon.

8:45 a.m.   Our executive committee meets to discuss the events of the past week and the business levels for the week ahead. Together we strategize, bounce ideas off each other, compare financial performance, and generally set our compass for the direction we want to be heading in.

10:30 a.m.   At reception, where a woman wants to use an old gift certificate for a spa package we no longer offer. Since the new packages are much more expensive, I negotiate with her and give her a deal that makes her happy and still makes us a bit of money. I head back to the office where a stack of mail, mainly from vendors with samples and brochures on new products, awaits me on my desk.

12:00 p.m.   Meet the spa's marketing advisor for lunch — she wants to find out from me how some of the advertising she has done is working, and if we need to make any changes to the marketing plan.

1:30 p.m.   Meet with our head therapist, who supervises all of the treatment staff and trains them on any new treatments. We need to review the spa menu and make changes before the menu gets reprinted next month. The final product is a negotiation between what I think I can sell, and what he thinks the staff will like to do.

2:30 p.m.   I go through a stack of that week's client comment cards. Most of them are positive and I write a thank-you note on each one and post them in the employee break room for the staff to see. The negative ones require a little more investigating. I call one guest to get more information and invite her back for a return visit. I send a letter to some of them thanking them for their feedback.

3:15 p.m.   A massage therapist comes to my office. She reveals that she is upset because she is not getting enough shifts on her schedule. Together, we review her schedule and look at some options for her to pick up more shifts. The therapists are the most important resource we have, so I do what I can to keep them happy.

4:15 p.m.   A writer calls wanting to interview me for an article in a local business magazine. I answer his questions and forward him some photographs to back up the article. It is good to get a phone call like that; it means our PR efforts are paying off! I end the day with a final walkthrough of the facility to check up on all the staff, and make sure the assistant spa director is ready to take over until closing. Time to go home, rest up and get ready for another busy day tomorrow!

2.1.3   The Owner's Role

The spa owner is responsible for all aspects of the business, although he or she may delegate actually doing some or all of the functions below.

- Ensuring that the spa is clean and the equipment is in working order

- Finding new ways to minimize costs and maximize revenue

- Supervising staff members or manager

- Assisting accountant with sorting out any issues

- Ensuring all certificates, licenses and accreditations spa and staff require are current

- Being highly visible and addressing guest concerns professionally

- Interviewing, hiring and training employees

- Scheduling staff appropriately

- Appraising performance, rewarding and disciplining employees

- Marketing the spa to new clients

You don't need to have worked for 20 years in the spa industry or be a slick business investor to succeed as a spa owner. The growth of the industry has created opportunities not only for experienced professionals who have been working at it for a while, but it also opens the door for people stepping into the spa business for the first time.

What you do need is enthusiasm, a desire to be in the spa environment on a daily basis, and a willingness to learn. A new spa is like a new child. It requires a lot of time, attention, and care for several years. Experts advise you get into this business because you love it, not for the money.

Lynne McNees, President of the International Spa Association, encourages people to use whatever experience they have to apply to spa leadership roles. "If you were the head of a department store, you would probably have the skills needed to succeed because you would have been taught incredible customer service, multi-tasking, management of people, management of budgets, etc. There are a lot of industries you could pull from that would make sense."

The Typical Spa Owner

Most people who decide to open a spa have a least a few of the following characteristics in common — see how many apply to you. While you certainly do not need to have all the characteristics mentioned below to become a spa owner, chances are if you are considering this business venture you'll see a reflection of yourself in these descriptions.

An appreciation of spas

Most people who decide to start a spa have visited a spa in the past year at least once, and came away with a sense of peace and well-being that a spa visit can bring. In order to sell a service such as spa treatments to clients, you need to believe that they are valuable and worthwhile. The more you can learn about spas and spa treatments before you launch your spa, the better prepared you'll be as owner to make key business decisions.

A belief in a mind-body-spirit connection

Many spa services are based on the premise that our mental state affects our physical health, and that to be wholly healthy, we need to heal ourselves in both realms. For this reason, many spa owners practice yoga, meditation, or have a holistic approach to their own health. Being in touch with your "spiritual side" does help!

A genuine enjoyment of people

This is a people-oriented business, so "people" people tend to do well. There are not many businesses (and even fewer legal ones) where the customers take off their clothes as soon as they get there! You will likely be the kind of person who enjoys telling people about wonderful experiences you have had, and hearing their stories as well. You feel a personal sense of pride whenever you can make people feel better. You're the kind of person people naturally open up to and trust.

Being cool under pressure

It is the personality and demeanor of the spa owner that helps create the relaxing ambience of the spa, and their experiential wisdom is what helps them make decisions and run a profitable business. "On the surface you want the spa to appear a calm, tranquil place," said ISPA President Lynne McNees, "but behind the scenes [you] need to jump into action and be able to deal with situations."

Basic business sense

As fun and funky as running a spa can be, remember that it is still a business. There is all the usual work like budgeting, hiring and training staff, as well as appointment-booking and managing an inventory of supplies and products, going to the bank and paying your bills on time. A good business sense from any industry can be applied to the spa industry. If this is not your thing, you'll want to make sure you have a manager or team member who will take care of these details for you, and explain them to you in ways you can make sense of.

Creativity

All business owners need a dash of creativity to set their services apart. You'll use your creativity to decorate your spa, come up with enticing names for your packages and services, and plan ways to market your spa to the public.

2.2 Spa Services

As owner you will have the creative challenge and fun of selecting the treatments your spa will offer. This mix can be as eclectic or straightforward as you want, but remember that for every service or treatment, you will have to have a staff member able and available to perform it. For this reason, many spa owners start off offering just the basics, and test out specialty treatments only a few at a time.

In the section below, we have focused on the basics as an introduction to what you may offer. You will learn who performs the service, approximately how long it usually takes, what supplies and equipment are required, what takes place, and a general idea of what you can charge for that service.

We also explain what the perceived benefits are of each treatment. In section 4.5 we'll take a look at building your selected treatments into a menu of services, where you'll market them to clients.

2.2.1   Massage Therapy

Whether it's the basic Swedish massage or newer techniques such as heated stone therapy and raindrop therapy, spa clientele come back again and again for the tension-relieving, soothing benefits of massage.

Swedish Massage

Performed By:	Massage therapist
Time Required:	1 hour
Equipment Used:	Massage table, light oils
Description:	A bit of oil is applied to client's head, hands and feet and gentle strokes and light pressure is administered. Oil is then applied to client's arms, legs, neck, back and shoulders and stronger massage strokes are applied.
Benefits:	Releases tension and stress, increases blood flow, reduces muscle soreness, relaxation
Approx. Retail Cost:	$75-$85

Deep Tissue or Sports Massage

Performed By:	Massage therapist
Time Required:	1 hour
Equipment Used:	Massage table, possibly a mix of pure, organic essential oils

Description:	An oiled or dry massage. If used, oil is applied to client's arms, neck, legs, and hands. Deep pressure is used on large and small muscles and at trigger points on the body. Pressure is applied with therapist's fingers, fists, and elbows. Client is turned over and oil is applied to back, neck and shoulders and deep massage strokes continue.
Benefits:	Balances nervous system, reduces muscle tension, promotes a feeling of well-being, relaxation
Approx. Retail Cost:	$75-$110

Aromatherapy Massage

Performed By:	Massage therapist
Time Required:	½ hour to 1 hour
Equipment Used:	Massage table, a mix of scented oils
Description:	Client may choose scented oil, or therapist may choose from popular choices such as citrus, coconut, mint, or floral. Oil is applied to client's arms, neck, legs, hands and feet and gentle strokes using light pressure is administered. Client breathes in the aroma and relaxes. Oil is applied to client's back and shoulders and light massage strokes are applied.
Benefits:	Balances nervous system, reduces muscle tension, promotes a feeling of well-being, relaxation
Approx. Retail Cost:	½ hour ($45-$60) or 1 hour ($70-$95)

Reflexology

Performed By:	Massage therapist
Time Required:	½ hour to 1 hour

Equipment Used:	Massage table, moisturizing gel
Description:	Many spas begin with a warm, fragranced foot bath. Then client reclines as a moisturizing gel is applied and therapist massages the feet with some light pressure, using thumbs and fingers. The entire foot from toes, to between the toes, to ball of the foot, to the heel of the foot is massaged. Each reflex point on the foot is touched, representing a different organ of the body.
Benefits:	Stimulates the nerve reflexes, relieves aching feet, total body relaxation
Approx. Retail Cost:	½ hour ($50) or 1 hour ($65-$100)

Hot Stone Massage

Performed By:	Massage therapist
Time Required:	1 hour to 1½ hours
Time Required:	Massage table, warm lava or basalt stones, gemstones or quartz crystals, and cold marble stones
Description:	Most often a combination of Swedish massage and heated stone therapy, basic massage strokes are applied all over client's body. Then, heated stones in varying sizes and shapes are placed at strategic points on client's body (forehead, hands, back, neck, arms, posterior, thighs, calves, even between toes). Varying degrees of heated temperatures and light to strong pressure are applied. Cold stones may then be applied to further the experience.
Benefits:	Alleviates pain and soreness, increases flexibility and blood flow, relaxation
Approx. Retail Cost:	1 hour ($80-$100); 1 ½ hours ($90-$125)

Thai Massage

Performed By:	Massage therapist
Time Required:	1 hour to 1½ hours
Equipment Used:	Yoga mat
Description:	Client sits on mat as therapist kneads and works back muscles with hands and feet. Client is moved in positions on the mat from lying on back, stomach and each side while therapist stretches muscles in a series of yoga-like movements and works pressure points on the shoulders, back and neck.
Benefits:	Alleviates pain and soreness, increases flexibility, stretches muscles, relaxation
Approx. Retail Cost:	1 hour ($100); 1 ½ hour ($140)

Raindrop Therapy

Performed By:	Massage therapist
Time Required:	1 hour to 1½ hours
Equipment Used:	Massage table, several pure, essential oils, hot towels
Description:	Client lies on stomach. Different essential oils are intermittently dispersed along the spine and back from an angle above the body. The feeling is that of lightly falling raindrops on the skin. Oils are lightly worked into the back and spine. Hot towels are applied to further relax the body.
Benefits:	Reduces muscle tension, promotes a feeling of well-being, relaxation
Approx. Retail Cost:	1 hour ($75-$85); 1 ½ hours ($100-$125)

Reiki Energy Therapy

Performed By: Certified Reiki therapist

Time Required: 1 hour to 1½ hours

Equipment Used: Massage table

Description: Therapist holds hands a few inches from client's body and moves hands along the body, which releases client's own life force and energy force. Process continues slowly over entire body. Therapist may chant slowly, as well. Therapist does not necessarily touch client, except maybe to gently cradle client's head in order to relax and center client's life force or to hold client's hands.

Benefits: Renewed energy, detoxified system, relaxation

Approx. Retail Cost: 1 hour ($70-$85), 1 ½ hours ($85-$125)

Rolfing Muscle Therapy

Performed By: Massage therapist

Time Required: 1 hour to 1½ hours

Equipment Used: Massage table, essential oils

Description: Client reclines. Client's muscles and tissues are then vigorously manipulated with deep massage. The body is then gradually and continually moved and rolled in a series of lengthening and stretching movements in an effort to reposition the body and put it back into alignment. Light oil massage may be included.

Benefits: Restores flexibility, improves posture, reduces muscle tension, relaxation

Approx. Retail Cost: $140

Ayurvedic

Performed By:	Massage therapist
Time Required:	1 hour
Equipment Used:	Massage table, herbs and essential oils specifically chosen for each client according to their body type
Description:	Client reclines while mix of herbs and heated oils are applied to hair and scalp and drizzled along meridian lines, or energy centers, of the body. One or two therapists work the oils into the scalp and body with light pressure and deep massage pressure at varying times. Two therapists will work in harmony to ensure true relaxation.
Benefits:	Reduced muscle tension promotes mental clarity, increased energy, feeling of well-being, relaxation
Approx. Retail Cost:	1 therapist ($110); 2 therapists ($220)

Pregnancy Massage

Performed By:	Massage therapist
Time Required:	1 hour to 1½ hours
Equipment Used:	Pregnancy massage table, light body oil
Description:	Usually administered after the first trimester, only gentle, easy strokes are used. Client lies on her stomach and oil is massaged over back, legs, and ankles. Client turns over, more oil is in-troduced and client is lightly massaged over shoulders, neck and head, with a special concentration on temples and back of the neck.

Benefits:	Reduces stress, improves circulation, alleviates swelling, cramping and headaches associated with pregnancy, relaxation
Approx. Retail Cost:	1 hour ($95-$120); 1 ½ hours ($125 and up)

Cranio-Sacral Massage

Performed By:	Massage therapist
Time Required:	½ hour to 1½ hours
Equipment Used:	Massage table, essential oils
Description:	Client reclines. Therapist drizzles oil a little at a time, starting at the shoulders, and moves on to the neck, head, scalp, temples and facial bones. Gentle massage, light touches and light tapping motions are used. Therapist may also ask client to imitate simple, rhythmic breathing techniques during the massage to relieve tension.
Benefits:	Enhances body functions, helps to alleviate headache pain, migraines and chronic neck and back pain, relaxation
Approx. Retail Cost:	½ hour ($50); 1 hour ($70-$85); 1 ½ hours ($95-$125)

2.2.2   Body Treatments

Body treatments get a little more "goopy" and they are usually defined more by the products used than they are by their techniques. These include body scrubs which can be done with sugars, salts, or other exfoliating products, and body wraps performed with seaweeds, mud, oils, lotions and more. Clients emerge polished, buffed, moisturized, relaxed and supremely pampered.

Body Polish or Salt Glow

Performed By:	Esthetician
Time Required:	½ hour to 1 hour
Equipment Used:	Massage table, body scrub and body cream. Some of the more popular body scrubs feature sea salt, crushed almonds, coffee granules, brown sugar, or crushed pearls. Popular body cream ingredients include honey, almond, ginger, coconut, lavender, peppermint, chocolate, or milk.
Description:	Client reclines while entire body is rubbed and exfoliated with selected scrub. Client then showers and dries off. A prepared lotion or cream is then smoothed on to finish the treat-ment.
Benefits:	Removes dead skin cells, incredibly silky smooth skin, relaxation
Approx. Retail Cost:	$55-$95

Body Wrap

Performed By:	Esthetician
Time Required:	Approx. 1 hour
Equipment Used:	Body scrub brush, mud, seaweed or oil-based lotion, body scrub and body cream
Description:	Treatment may begin with gentle body brush exfoliation or a body scrub on arms, legs, back, and torso. Mud, seaweed or oil-based lotion is applied. Common choices may include seaweed (detoxifying), citrus (invigorating), herbal, such as green tea or lavender (relaxing), mud or aloe vera (moisturizing). Client is wrapped in plastic and relaxes for 20 minutes on heated table, then

plastic is removed and client showers. Chosen moisturizer is then applied.

Benefits: Removes dead skin cells, silky-smooth skin, relaxation

Approx. Retail Cost: $55-$95

Body Scrub & Steam

Performed By: Esthetician

Time Required: 1 hour

Equipment Used: Steam room, body brush or body scrub, body lotion, cream or body butter, towels

Description: Client's hair is wrapped in a towel. Client's arms, legs, back, and torso are gently buffed with body brush or body scrub or both. Coffee, sea salt or sugar-based scrubs are preferred. Client then showers and is wrapped in a towel. Client is led to steam room to relax for 15 to 20 minutes. A moisturizing, scented lotion or body butter is applied.

Benefits: Removes dead skin cells, silky-smooth skin, relaxation

Approx. Retail Cost: $55-$95

Seaweed Body Peel

Performed By: Esthetician

Time Required: 50 minutes

Equipment Used: Vichy shower table, body brush, seaweed sheets, oil or lotion

Description: Client showers, then reclines on table as legs, arms and torso are exfoliated with body brush.

Seaweed sheets are placed on the body. Vichy shower's light, warm mist wets the seaweed sheets. Client relaxes for 30 minutes. Seaweed sheets are gently removed and lotion or oil of choice is applied.

Benefits: Detoxifies, firms, exfoliates, incredibly silky-smooth skin, relaxation

Approx. Retail Cost: $150

Mud Bath

Performed By: Esthetician

Time Required: 50 minutes

Equipment Used: Tub, clay mud, shower, steam room, warm blanket or towel, essential oils or lotion

Description: Client relaxes in mud-filled tub for 15 minutes as mud coats entire body, then client rinses off in a hot mineral water shower. Client enters steam room for relaxing steam, (approx. 5 minutes). Client is then wrapped in warm, aromatic blanket or towel for 5 minutes. Treatment concludes with 15-minute massage with choice of essential oils.

Benefits: Detoxifies, exfoliates, silky-soft skin, relaxation

Approx. Retail Cost: $80-$100

2.2.3   Hydrotherapy

Once known as "taking the waters", hydrotherapy treatments have always been popular with spa-goers for their cleansing, healing, nurturing, and almost womb-like experience. Many spas offer water treatments not only on a treatment table but also in a hydrotherapy tub. If your budget allows this opens up a range of new services you can offer, but they range in cost from approximately $10,000 to $30,000, and so is not a possible offering for all start-up spas.

Watsu (Water Massage Therapy)

Performed By: Massage therapist

Time Required: 1 hour

Equipment Used: Tub with warm water

Description: Client is treated to a combination of hydro-therapy and shiatsu massage. Client is sub-merged in water as therapist moves client's body in a rhythmic motion along the water. Thera-pist then uses a series of stretching motions on client's arms, legs, back and neck, moving them through the water. A series of long massage strokes and muscle manipulations follow, with light and strong massage pressure used.

Benefits: Reduced muscle tension, tranquility, relaxation

Approx. Retail Cost: $95

Thalasso Bath Therapy

Performed By: Spa technician or esthetician

Time Required: ½ hour

Equipment Used: Tub with power jets and warm water infused with seaweed, mineral oils, scented oils or bath salts

Description: Client relaxes in tub as 60 or more invigorating power jets circulate throughout, naturally mas-saging and stimulating muscles. A light mas-sage or body scrub may precede this treatment.

Benefits: Detoxifies, reduces muscle tension, relaxation

Approx. Retail Cost: $75

Jantzu

Performed By:	Massage therapist
Time Required:	45 minutes
Equipment Used:	Warm water or salt water pool or tub
Description:	Client relaxes in pool or tub filled with chest-high water as therapist cradles client under the arms and administers a series of gentle rolling and rocking motions through the water. This continues as therapist uses stretching techniques and gently supports, lightly massages and maneuvers client's body through the water.
Benefits:	Relieves muscle soreness, feeling of well-being, relaxation
Approx. Retail Cost:	$90

Vichy Water Treatment

Performed By:	Esthetician
Time Required:	1 hour
Equipment Used:	Vichy shower table, sea salt or sugar scrub, essential oils
Description:	Client reclines on table as arms, legs, and torso are rubbed with scrub. Client then relaxes as the warm, light mist of the Vichy shower sprays the body. Client towels off and skin is smoothed with prepared oils.
Benefits:	Stimulates circulation, silky-soft skin, relaxation
Approx. Retail Cost:	$100-$125

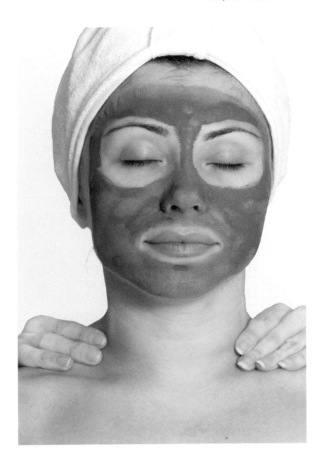

2.2.4 Facials

The mainstay of any type of spa today, facials seek to rejuvenate, hydrate, smooth and energize the skin. Niche facials growing in popularity are teen and men's care facials, and advanced anti-aging treatments.

Medical esthetician services may also be offered for more scientific skin treatment of the face and body. Estheticians are most well known for doing facials but also perform treatments for more specific skin ailments such as acne, cellulite and, of course, wrinkles.

European Facial

Performed By: Esthetician

Time Required:	½ hour to 1 hour
Equipment Used:	Special lighting, steam machine, extraction tools, cleansers, peels or masks, ampoules, toners, moisturizers
Description:	Esthetician analyzes skin type and instructs on the proper care of skin and proper products to use. Client reclines. Proper deep pore cleanser for skin type is applied and wiped off. A light scented steam is then introduced to open pores and relax client. Extractions are performed. Personalized repair or re-moisturizing ampoules are applied. Light facial and neck massage follows. Mask or enzyme peel for skin type is applied. Client relaxes for approx. ten minutes. Mask or peel is removed and clarifying toner applied. Moisturizer for skin type follows.
Benefits:	Exfoliates, restores skin's health, satin-smooth skin, relaxation
Approx. Retail Cost:	$60-$120

Mini-Facial (Cucumber)

Performed By:	Esthetician
Time Required:	30-35 minutes
Equipment Used:	Special lighting, warm towels, cleanser, peel or mask, cucumbers
Description:	Client reclines and cucumber-based cleanser is applied and wiped off. Cucumber mask or peel is applied. Client relaxes for approx. 5 minutes. Warm towels are applied to remove mask or peel. Light facial massage follows. Cucumber slices are applied and client relaxes for 5 minutes. Cucumber slices are removed.

Benefits:	Restores skin's health, relaxation
Approx. Retail Cost:	$70

Anti-Aging Facial

Performed By:	Esthetician
Time Required:	1 hour
Equipment Used:	Special lighting, steam machine, extraction tools, cleanser, AHA peel, mask, ampoules or moistur-izers
Description:	Client reclines. Esthetician analyzes skin type and instructs on the proper care of skin and proper products to use. An ultra-moisturizing cleanser is applied and wiped off. Steam is then introduced to open pores and relax client. Extraction is performed, if necessary. Peel or mask is applied. Popular types include gentle AHA peel, collagen sheet mask, oxygenating mask or marine caviar and crushed pearl mask. Client relaxes for 10 minutes and peel or mask is removed. A light facial massage may follow. Repairing Vitamin C ampoule or creamy moisturizer is spread on the skin to complete the facial.
Benefits:	Refines skin texture, silky-smooth skin, restores skin's health, hydration, relaxation
Approx. Retail Cost:	$100 and up

Teen Facial

Performed By:	Esthetician
Time Required:	1 hour
Equipment Used:	Special lighting, steam machine, extraction tools, cleansers, peels or masks, toners, lotions

Description:	Esthetician analyzes skin type and instructs client on the proper care of skin and proper products to use. Client reclines and proper cleanser for skin type is applied and wiped off. Steam is then introduced to open pores and relax client. Extraction of whiteheads or blackheads is performed. Peel or mask for skin type will be applied. Client will then relax for approx. ten minutes with mask on. Mask is removed and clarifying toner applied. A light moisturizer or lotion may then be applied, if necessary.
Benefits:	Learn proper skin care, restores skin's health, relaxation
Approx. Retail Cost:	$85 and up

Gentleman's Facial

Performed By:	Esthetician
Time Required:	1 hour
Equipment Used:	Special lighting, steam machine, extraction tools, cleansers, peels or masks, toners, lotions
Description:	Esthetician analyzes skin type. Client reclines and proper cleanser for skin type is applied and wiped off. Steam is then introduced to open pores and relax client. Extraction of whiteheads or blackheads is performed. Peel or mask is applied. Client then relaxes for approx. ten minutes with mask on. Mask is removed and clarifying toner applied. A light facial and neck massage follows. A light moisturizer or lotion may then be applied.
Benefits:	Calms razor burn sensitivity, restores skin's health, relaxation
Approx. Retail Cost:	$85 and up

2.2.5 Beauty/Salon Services

Traditional waxing services are still offered at spas around the world, but laser hair removal is becoming popular because it promises a permanent, virtually pain-free solution to unwanted facial or body hair.

Many spa owners consider that makeup application after a facial or hair care service coupled with those little extra beauty treatments, fully complete their service offerings.

Nail care is a basic service offered at most spas. They may include acrylic nail tip and nail wrap services and French manicures and pedicures. Many spas employ hair stylists and colorists to help clients look and feel their best. Some spas provide a complimentary shampoo and style service after a facial.

Spa Manicure

Performed By: Nail technician

Time Required: 30 to 45 minutes

Equipment Used: Manicure table and chair, manicure tools, scrub, lotion, oil, warm towels, nail polish remover, nail polish, nail dryer

Description: Client's hands are washed with warm towel. Nail polish remover is used and nails are filed or clipped to desired length. Hands are rubbed with fine granular scrub and client washes them off at the sink. Hands and fingers are then massaged with lotion or cream. Then fingertips are placed in warm, soapy water. Once each hand is removed and dried, cuticle oil is rubbed in and cuticles are pushed back or trimmed. Base coat polish is applied to both hands, then two coats of color polish of the client's choice are applied and finally a topcoat polish is applied. Client then rests fingertips in a nail dryer or allows nails to dry naturally for 15-20 minutes. Light neck and shoulder massage may be included.

Benefits:	Beautifies nails, repairs cuticles, smoothes hands, relaxation
Approx. Retail Cost:	$20 to $40 (French manicure, add $5-$10)

Spa Pedicure

Performed By:	Nail technician
Time Required:	½ hour to 45 minutes
Equipment Used:	Pedicure seat and basin, pedicure tools, tissue strips, paper sandals, scrub, lotion, oil, warm towels, nail polish
Description:	Client's feet are placed in foot tub with warm, soapy water. Feet are rubbed with a pumice stone, placed in soapy water again and dried. Toenails are filed or clipped to desired length. Scrub is applied and massaged in. Feet are placed back in tub to be cleansed again. Foot is dried, lotions or creams are applied and massaged in, then that foot is placed in sandals and tissue strips are wrapped between the toes. Cuticle oil is rubbed in, cuticles pushed back or clipped. Base coat, two coats of color polish, and topcoat are applied. (Light foot massage may be included before polishes are applied.)
Benefits:	Beautifies feet, smoothes feet, relaxation
Approx. Retail Cost:	$40 to $60 (French pedicure, add $5-$10)

Paraffin Wax Treatment

Performed By:	Nail technician
Time Required:	½ hour
Equipment Used:	Manicure table and chair or pedicure seat, heated hand or foot tub, warm towel, paraffin wax, lotion

Description:	Client's hands or feet are cleansed with warm towel or washed in sink or basin, then fully dried. One hand or foot is lowered into warm paraffin wax and dipped in and out two or three times. The procedure is repeated with the other hand or foot. Client relaxes for 5 to 10 minutes and paraffin wax is removed. A moisturizing lotion may be applied and massaged in.
Benefits:	Smoothes hands and feet, relaxation
Approx. Retail Cost:	$15 to $20

Hair Cut or Style

Performed By:	Licensed hair stylist

Time Required:	30 minutes
Equipment Used:	Shampoo, hair conditioner, towels, scissors, blow-dryer, curling iron, hair brushes and combs, rollers, styling products
Description:	Client's hair is washed and conditioned, and head lightly massaged. Hair is towel dried. Stylist cuts, styles or curls hair according to client's desired look. Styling products are applied. Client's hair is blow-dried and hair spray may be added.
Benefits:	New, clean look
Approx. Retail Cost:	$20 to $125

Hair Coloring or Highlights

Performed By:	Licensed colorist
Time Required:	1 hour or more
Equipment Used:	Shampoo, hair conditioner, towels, caps, color dyes or glosses, bleach, foil brush, foils, blow-dryer, hair brushes, combs, styling products
Description:	Color is mixed and applied to client's hair. For highlighting, hair strands are either pulled through a cap or placed on foils and bleach solution is brushed on. Client relaxes for approx. 20 to 30 minutes. Solution is shampooed out. Conditioner is applied and washed out. Hair is styled as desired.
Benefits:	Newer, younger look, conditioned hair
Approx. Retail Cost:	$55 to $125

Permanent (Perm)

Performed By:	Licensed hair stylist
Time Required:	1 ½ hours to 2 hours

Equipment Used:	Towels, perm solution and bottle, perm rods, perm cloths, blow-dryer, hair brushes and combs, styling products
Description:	Client's hair is sectioned off and rolled around perm rods. Perming solution is squirted on through bottle nozzle. Perm cloths are wrapped around perm rods. Client relaxes for 20 minutes under hooded heated dryer. Solution is then rinsed out with water. Hair is towel-dried and styled as desired.
Benefits:	Soft curls or waves in hair
Approx. Retail Cost:	$65 and up

Deep Conditioning Treatment

Performed By:	Licensed hair stylist
Time Required:	30 minutes
Equipment Used:	Shampoo, deep conditioner, towels, blow-dryer, hair brushes and combs, styling products
Description:	Client's hair is shampooed. Deep conditioner is applied. Client's hair is wrapped in plastic, then client sits under hooded heat dryer for approximately 20 minutes. Client's hair is shampooed again, and then styled as desired.
Benefits:	No split ends, silky-soft, ultra-conditioned hair
Approx. Retail Cost:	$40 and up

Lip Treatment

Performed By:	Esthetician
Time Required:	15 minutes
Equipment Used:	Moist towel, light granule scrub, moisturizing lip balm

Description:	Client reclines while lips are gently exfoliated with scrub, possibly fruit-based. Scrub is removed with moist towel. Moisturizing, nutrient-rich lip balm is applied.
Benefits:	Smooth, moisturized lips
Approx. Retail Cost:	$25 and up

Skin Bronzing or Golden Glow Tan

Performed By:	Esthetician or certified airbrush tanning technician
Time Required:	1 hour
Equipment Used:	Body scrub, self-tanning lotion or cream
Description:	Client showers, dries off completely. Client's body is exfoliated with chosen body scrub, most likely coffee, sea salt or sugar based. Client showers again. Client's body is smoothed all over with self-tanning lotion or cream with a glove, or tan is airbrushed on. Client is usually asked not to shower again for 8 to 24 hours.
Benefits:	Smooth, healthy-looking skin, "sun-kissed" tan without the sun
Approx. Retail Cost:	$140

Body and Facial Waxing

Performed By:	Cosmetologist
Time Required:	15 to 30 minutes
Equipment Used:	Table, tub or basin, waxes, waxing sticks, waxing strips, lotion
Description:	Cosmetologist puts on protective gloves. Client reclines as warm wax is applied to area with a stick. Client can opt for full face or body, eyebrow,

upper lip, chin, back, shoulders, half arm or full arm, half leg, full leg, bikini or Brazilian bikini hair removal. Strip is placed over the wax and gently, but quickly, pulled away. A soothing lotion is then applied to condition the area.

Benefits: Smooth, hairless face and body, renewed confidence

Approx. Retail Cost: From $15 to $100

Laser Hair Removal

Performed By: Licensed nurse or physician

Time Required: 15 minutes to 1 hour

Equipment Used: Table, laser equipment, protective eyeglasses or eye mask, anesthetic gel or cream

Description: Client prepares area prior to treatment and removes any deodorant, powder or makeup. Client may choose lip, chin, underarm, face, neck, bikini area, legs, or back for treatment. Client receives consultation, may fill out forms, and is given post-treatment instruction. Client is given protective eyewear and reclines. Cream or gel is applied, if necessary. Gentle, pulsing laser light beam is introduced.

Benefits: Smooth, hairless face and body, renewed confidence

Approx. Retail Cost: From $750 to $2,500 for 5 treatments

Makeup Application

Performed By: Cosmetologist

Time Required: ½ hour

Equipment Used: Makeup, makeup brushes and sponges

Description:	Client's face will be prepared with foundation for skin tone and skin type, under-eye concealer will be applied. Then the proper blush will be swept across the cheekbones. Base eye shadow will be applied, followed by one to two blended and complementary eye shadows. Eye pencil or liquid eye liner is then applied. An eyelash curler may be used, topped off with one to two coats of mascara.
Benefits:	Beautiful results, prepared for social engagements
Approx. Retail Cost:	Complimentary with a facial, or from $40 and up

Other Treatments to Consider

Depending on the type of spa you decide to open, you may want to add to the treatments listed here with something more suited to your specialty. For example, an anti-aging spa (one of the hot trends today) may choose to add Botox treatments or skin peels performed by an RN.

If the spa has fitness facilities a wealth of other services may be offered, including fitness classes, personal fitness instruction, and private sessions in yoga, tai chi, or pilates. In a holistic spa, the services offered can get much more esoteric, often based on eastern philosophies including meditation, acupuncture or acupressure, aromatherapy treatments, and even ear candling.

Every spa, whether it is a day spa, a resort spa or a destination spa, has signature specialty treatments that appeal to clientele for their uniqueness and ability to relax and pamper like nothing else. Part of designing your business plan (see section 3.3) will involve the development of your spa's signature treatments.

These may incorporate unique items or ingredients such as fresh rose or other flower petals, chocolate, yogurt, any number of different aromatherapy experiences, exotic muds, or they may focus on a newly discovered (or newly trendy) technique in massage or healing. Your imagination is really your only limit!

2.3 Get Ready to Own a Spa

"Do as much research [and] read as many articles as you can. Really know the technical parts of the job. Be informed of the trends, visit spas."

— *Lori Hutchinson, Hutchinson Consulting*

While you are getting ready to own and possibly manage your spa, there are many skills you can work on developing early that will help you be more successful. All of these skills can be learned, and not necessarily in a classroom, either.

Now that you understand what the spa environment is like, you can begin to focus more clearly on developing your skills through both conventional and unconventional ways, as this section will explain.

2.3.1 Do a Personal Inventory

In order to evaluate what spa owner skill areas you are going to want to develop, it's best to start by doing an inventory of where your skills are already well developed. John Korpi, founder of SpaQuest International and current President of the ISPA Foundation, told us he breaks the skill sets for the spa industry into the following categories:

- Reception/Administration

- Treatments, Skin Care, and Massage

- Salon (Hair and Nails)

- Fitness

- Nutrition/Cuisine

- Lifestyle Counseling and Mind-Body Disciplines

- Retail and Product Development

- Financial Business Management

- Marketing and Public Relations

Korpi suggests that someone who will be running a spa should be an expert in two or three of these areas, and then look for educational opportunities in the others. By breaking the career into bite-sized pieces, it is easier to take personal inventory of where your skills and experience lie and where you need additional training.

Not all these skill areas apply to every type of spa — for example, unless you are going to offer nutritional counseling or fitness classes, it is okay to focus your energies elsewhere. Of course, the best way to learn is by doing. For that reason, direct spa experience is important, but it is important to understand how your other experiences can make you a qualified candidate for spa ownership.

The spa business is so vast and covers so many broad areas that, regardless of your background and experience, you can probably apply it in some way. Do a quick analysis of the different kinds of work and career experience you have had and see what parts of your work history fit into the following categories.

Retail Experience

One of the biggest potential revenue generators in any spa is their sale of retail products, gifts and clothing. If you have a background in retail, you are bringing a lot of desirable experience to the table. Some spa experts say that a spa should be making as much as 25% of their income from retail sales.

While these benchmarks of one-to-one retail revenue to treatment revenue ratios are often quoted by industry experts in trade magazines, spa director Jeremy McCarthy assures us that in reality, most spas are making only ten percent of their revenue from retail sales. Five to ten percent would be a reasonable figure to shoot for, again depending on your spa's style and niche, and a retail background will give you a foothold in understanding how to achieve this.

Administrative/Clerical Experience

Running a busy spa means running a busy office. Phones are ringing, appointments have to be made accurately and efficiently, and the staff will be coordinating all the comings and goings of the customers. An owner who has experience running a busy office, handling multi-line phones, making a schedule, keeping a busy staff well trained and organized, etc. can hit the ground running in this business.

Certain administrative experiences can be even more useful. A hotel reservations manager, for example, can bring a wealth of knowledge about how to maximize the appointment bookings on any given day, which directly affects the profitability of the spa.

Sales, Marketing and PR Experience

A sales and marketing background can be a huge plus in running a spa. Someone with this background might eliminate the necessity of paying someone else a hefty amount of money to market your spa.

Creativity is a key trait for spa owners. They need to be able to create an extensive treatment menu that will appeal to their customers, so they should have writing skills to be able to describe these treatments, and will need to come up with a presentation in the form of a printed menu or brochure to show off what the spa has to offer.

Once the menu is created and the spa is up and running, the owner will need to keep up with the trends and continually adapt to the needs of their customers. They will have to keep their spa fresh in the minds of their patrons with promotional events and activities and further printed material.

The hands-on owner must also develop a relationship with the media, and get their spa featured in the press as much as possible. This might mean writing your own press releases or, at the very least, giving your PR people information with the necessary "wow factor" so they can create a press release which will be worthy of landing on an editor's desk.

Accounting Experience

Accounting and finance is another area that is essential to the profitability of the spa, and yet is a weak area for many spa owners. Sometimes owners or directors have difficulty directly relating the financial performance of the spa to how it is managed and operated. A financially knowledgeable business manager is able to make these connections, and respond in meaningful ways. For example, if one treatment has a very high cost of labor and goods, and/or is not that popular, it will be time to respond by replacing it with a less expensive or more popular option.

Hospitality Experience

Of course the spa business has always been tied to the hospitality industry because of the number of spas located in hotels and resorts. Regardless of the spa's location, hospitality experience brings important knowledge about how to treat your customers.

Customers go to a spa to be taken care of, and they expect to feel that level of caring from every employee they meet, not only their massage therapist. A successful spa will make its guests feel welcome and safe from the stresses of the outside world.

In the hospitality industry, one learns all the tenets of excellent customer service, skills that can greatly enhance the spa experience or a customer. Even the slightest glitch in customer service can greatly disrupt the relaxation level of a guest in the spa.

"I have seen countless customers who choose not to go to a spa with the most extensive facilities in favor of one with the best customer service," says contributing author Jeremy McCarthy.

2.3.2   Courses and Seminars

Cornell University paved the way to spa leadership education 20 years ago, by developing a single course in spa management as part of their Hotel program — in fact, the program is still offered today. Now more and more schools and programs are being developed to help future spa owners and directors educate themselves on how to better run their business.

Whether a formal education in spa management is right for you depends on what you came up with in your skills inventory, as well as your availability of free time and money. If you found that you are lacking general business or specific spa management knowledge, and are in a position to attend school part time or full time, you can look into some of these better known spa management programs listed in this section.

Elmcrest College of Applied Arts and Sciences

Website: **www.elmcrestcollege.com/spa_management/ curriculum.asp**

Phone: 1-888-641-6300

About: Toronto, Canada's Elmcrest College of Applied Health Sciences and Spa Management has two programs of interest in Spa Management, in addition to a complementary course in spa customer service, and shorter certificate programs. Both programs are offered starting each September and January.

- *The Spa Manager-Director Program:* Provides the "skills necessary to meet the daily and long-term challenges of management within today's spa environment." Class hours total 1040 (ten months).

- *The Spa Leadership Program:* "Develops the skills required to manage day-to-day spa operations." Class hours total 720 (six months).

Arizona State University

Website: **www.poly.asu.edu/ecollege/wellness/spa/**

Phone: (480) 727-1945

About: The ASU Spa Management Certificate consists of 34 hours of coursework followed by a required 300 hour-internship at a spa. Coursework in the program combines exercise and wellness aspects with business training.

University of Derby

Website: **www.derby.ac.uk/international-spa-management-bsc-hons**

Phone: +44 (0)1298 71100

| *About:* | Based in the spa town of Buxton in England, U of D offers a unique 4-year Bachelor of Science degree program in International Spa Management that includes outplacement work programs as well as classroom study. You can also get credit for qualifications and skills you may have already developed in the work place. |

UC Irvine Extension

Website:	**http://unex.uci.edu/certificates/business_mgmt/ mgmt_supervisory_skills/spa/**
Phone:	(949) 824-5414
About:	This Spa and Hospitality Management Certificate Program is endorsed by the Day Spa Association and the International Medical Spa Association. A certificate is awarded upon completion of five required courses and two electives; however, you are free to take any courses you wish on an individual basis instead without enrolling in the certificate program. Cost of each course ranges from $495 to $625 U.S.

Short Training Courses and Seminars

You can also check with the hospitality program of the closest university, or use an education portal website to search for "spa management." Two such sites are the Education Portal at **http://education-portal. com/spa_management.html** and Peterson's Education Portal at **www. petersons.com/ugchannel**. At the time of publication, seven U.S. schools listed post-secondary education programs in Spa Management.

If you don't have a spa management program close to where you live, you can also take more general courses in hospitality management, as well as courses on starting and running a business. Check with your local community or vocational college to see what is available.

Alternately, you might also investigate shorter certificate programs or even weekend seminars on spa-related topics. They are also a good chance to meet a few industry experts and colleagues who you can network with in the future. We have listed a few of the better-known programs below.

Erica Miller Spa School

Website: **www.ericamillerspaschool.com**

Phone: 1-800-249-9618; 250-791-5563

About: Located in British Columbia, Canada, The Erica Miller Spa School offers a five-day Spa Director's Training Course in the spring and fall of each year. Topics include hiring, operations, choosing equipment and supplies, and profitability. Tuition is approximately $1,000 CDN. There are also assorted workshops on specific spa topics available on a regular basis.

Preston Wynne Success Systems

Website: **www.wynnebusiness.com**

Phone: 1-877-256-3513

About: Preston Wynne currently offers two spa start-up and management seminars, held in Pennsylvania and California a few times a year:

- *Spa Director's Management Intensive:* A four-day seminar covering financial management, marketing, service programs and packages, leadership, management, and retail success. Cost is $1,899 U.S.

- *Real World Spa Startup/Expansion Workshop:* A two-day workshop covering a variety of topics relating to building or expanding a spa operation. Cost is $999 U.S.

Preston Spa Business Solutions

Website: **www.psbsolutions.net**

Phone: 1-800-766-0375

About: Based in California, Douglas Preston's spa consulting company offers a two-day seminar called Sure Success for Starting a Spa. Topics include spa design and layout, service menus, and management issues. Cost is $999 U.S. There is also a separate two-day seminar available on marketing your spa for $495 U.S.

Salon Business Strategies

Website: **www.strategies.com/lefttext.php/sid/3**

Phone: 1-800-417-4848

About: Salon Business Strategies has an array of seminars that teach cutting edge business strategies for salons and spas. They are based in Connecticut and also offer some courses online. Current spa-focused offerings include Salon and Spa Manager Success Training ($695 U.S.); How Salons and Spas Make Money (online - $75); and Perfecting Your Salon/Spa Phone Scripts (online - $75).

Study from Home

The ISPA also offers spa management training in the form of nine study-at-home workbooks and a take-home exam. Called the Supervisory Skill Builders Workbooks, topics of study include Leadership, Communications, Time Management, Motivation, etc. The first one, "You as a Supervisor", focuses on basic supervisory skills.

The books cost $125 U.S. for ISPA members ($250 non-members) and the exam is an additional $100 ($200 non-members). Successful completion of the exam earns you the title of ISPA Certified Spa Supervisor.

2.3.3   Industry Conferences

The International Spa Association is the leading professional organization for the spa industry, with a membership of more than 2,300 health and wellness facilities and providers from 70 countries. The ISPA hosts the largest spa industry event of the year, the annual ISPA Conference, where you can attend seminars on cutting-edge business trends, techniques and innovations in the industry.

Lynne McNees, the ISPA President, says: "At the conference we offer 'Spa 101' programs to help the newcomers gain the knowledge they need to be successful — just one of several categories of educational programs offered at the conference. We try to give training and education at all levels."

The main annual event, the ISPA Conference and Expo, is held in a different location in the U.S. each year. The ISPA also helps organize "knowledge networks" across the country and throughout the year, where spa professionals can get together and share ideas. They keep an up-to-date schedule of these events on their website at **www.experienceispa.com/ISPA/Events**.

The Day Spa Association posts a list of industry trade shows on their website at **www.dayspaassociation.com/mainpages/tradeshows.htm**.

Leading Spas of Canada hosts an annual national conference attended by hundreds of people from within the industry. Laura Fluter, past LSC Executive Director, says that the conference is the premier event for those in the spa and wellness business, or those considering entering the industry, to tap into the latest trends, hear industry-leading speakers, and network with other spa professionals from around the world. For information visit **www.leadingspasofcanada.com/conference**.

2.3.4   Learn on Your Own

In addition to or in place of formal study, you can use any and all of the following routes to learn about the spa industry before you jump into it. In particular, finding a mentor or advisor can be an invaluable source of help, not just now but when you have questions once you are running your spa.

Read About Spas

The Internet abounds with spa-related websites, many geared towards educating spa professionals. Spa trade magazines are also a good source of information but even consumer publications seem to share a lot of "insider" information on the spa world.

As you start your research into the industry, try as much as possible to find information that is directed to you as an owner, rather than about how to do the job you'll pay staff to do. Although all that information is important, there is a limit to what you can reasonably expect to absorb, so you'll have to be choosy at times.

For example, you might not know how to give a massage yourself, but you should know how to receive a massage. What makes a good massage? Learn as much as you can about retail selling as well, since your staff will likely rely on your expertise in this area.

A list of helpful websites and publications can be found at the end of this guide to launch you on your quest for all things "spa."

Join an Association

Another source of industry information and networking opportunities is joining a professional association for those who work in or own spas.

A general membership in the ISPA is available to spas under development that plan to open within two years, or individuals wishing to expand their spa industry knowledge. A one-year general membership ranges in price from $510 to $892 U.S., and includes the company plus one primary member. Additional memberships can be purchased for $175. For information visit the International Spa Association (ISPA) at **www. experienceispa.com**.

The Day Spa Association offers industry news and trends information in the form of confidential reports and a quarterly newsletter. When your spa is ready to open they provide everything you need to identify yourself as a member to your clients, and a listing in their member directory. Memberships range in price from $155 to $225 per year. For information, you can visit **www.dayspaassociation.com/mainpages/spaprofessionals.htm**.

You can also visit The Spa Association at **www.thespaassociation.com** and the International Medical Spa Association at **www.medicalspa association.org** to learn what they have to offer you and your spa.

Leading Spas of Canada is the country's only national spa association, representing more than 150 spa and wellness centers. An annual general membership costs $600 and includes a listing in the membership directory, as well as a membership certificate to assure your clients that your spa adheres to membership standards. Other membership packages start at $3,000 and include the benefits of several marketing initiatives. For information visit **www.leadingspasofcanada.org**.

2.3.5   Get Some Spa Experience

Sometimes the best way to get to the top is by starting at the bottom. Depending on your background, skills and experience, you may have a lot to learn before you can assume a management position in the spa. By getting into the industry, you put yourself into a position to learn crucial aspects of spa management.

The front desk is like the central nervous system of the spa. It is from this point that all traffic, both people and information, flows in and out. Working in the reception area you will learn about your guests and customers, develop customer service skills and learn how to handle complaints.

You will learn about and interact with all staff in the spa, become familiar with the treatment menus, learn the computer systems and accounting procedures, and learn about retail products, selling and the point-of-sale system. From this vantage point, you will also observe how the spa director and other managers handle a variety of situations and you will be able to provide them support while learning a great deal.

Of course, not everyone can drop what they are doing and jump into a full-time or part-time job as a spa receptionist. If you aren't in a position to take advantage of this opportunity, you could also contact the spa manager about doing a day of job shadowing, or coming in for an interview instead.

The easiest way to find a job is to look for advertised positions. You can start with the links listed below. Many jobs these days go unadvertised, so you should also listen to the rumor mill. Talk to the employees at local spas. There is a lot that happens before a job is finally posted. Co-workers may know when someone is leaving long before they ever give their notice.

- *ISPA Job Bank*
  www.experienceispa.com/ISPA/Jobs

- *Spa Employment Bank*
  www.dayspaassociation.com/employment/employment.htm

- *Hcareers*
  www.hcareers.com

- *Hospitality Online*
  www.hospitalityonline.com

- *Spa Jobs*
  www.spa-jobs.com

- *Spas In Canada Classifieds*
  www.spasincanada.ca/spa_classifieds.html

- *Leading Spas of Canada – Career Opportunities*
  www.leadingspasofcanada.org/index.php?
  option=com_jobline&Itemid=92

2.3.6   Find a Mentor or Consultant

Another avenue to self-education is to find a spa owner, director or consultant who might be willing to take you under their wing and mentor you.

One of the contributors to this guide recently matched up a friend who was considering launching a new business with someone who had already opened a business in that industry. She was surprised how easily it came together.

"All it took was a simple email to get the ball rolling. I made sure the expert was open to doing some mentoring, and then got his phone number to give to my friend. By the next week I had heard they had been in contact several times, and that my friend was making plans to fly down to Colorado and spend a day onsite at the business.

"Now my friend is on the verge of finalizing his financing and setting up the business, and he may even name one of his products after that first mentor. You should not underestimate other people's willingness to help, and the value of the information they can provide!"

"Networking with other spa owners and bodyworkers has helped our business to thrive," says Jonathan Kenyon (manager of Apollo Day Spa in Waterville, Maine) in an online article published in Massage Magazine. "Not only do they help with generating industry resources, they place a more human face on the whole money-and-business component of owning a spa that can become draining." You can read the entire article online at **www.massagemag.com/spa/talk/openSpa.php**.

How to Make Contact

To find spa owners to contact, one of the best ways is to browse websites of spas until you find one that catches your eye. When you are looking for a potential mentor, the best choice would be someone who is running a spa that is as similar as possible in concept to what you have planned. If you want to open a mobile spa, you don't need to know the ins and outs of leasing from a brick-and-mortar spa owner, but you may want to ask how much to expect to budget each month for gasoline.

Of course, not everyone will be willing to help you out, especially if they feel like you will be in direct competition with their business. It's often best to look for mentors outside your immediate area, because let's face it: a spa in Seattle is not going to steal clients from one in Dallas.

> **TIP:** Remember that the basic tenets of doing business in each state are the same, but the regulations will vary. Make sure you are familiar with local licensing requirements.

Start by politely contacting the spa professional by email or phone. Explain to them that you are thinking of starting a spa, and that you greatly admire the way they are running theirs. Then ask if they have 15 minutes or so to spend answering a few questions you have about the business.

Respect that these people are as busy as you want to be some day, and find out what would be a good time to call or stop by if they are not too far away. You could also ask for an email address if that would be more convenient for them.

Here is a sample of a polite letter requesting an interview with a possible mentor:

Sample Request Letter

Dear Sandra Spa-Owner,

My name is Wanda Wannabe. I am doing research online about opening a spa because I am planning on launching such a business here in New Orleans. I found your website while doing a quick search of spas, and was extremely impressed with your spa's website. In particular, the unique treatments you offer and your stated commitment to service really caught my eye.

I am looking for an expert spa professional who wouldn't mind answering a couple of questions I have about launching this business. From the look of your website and a glance at some of the pictures of your spa in operation, I would be lucky to get a chance to speak with you.

If you would be willing to answer a couple of questions for me, I would truly appreciate it. I can call you, or if you prefer, I can correspond with you by email or whatever works for you. Please let me know if you would be willing to speak with me. Thank you in advance for your time.

Sincerely,

Wanda Wannabe
Phone: (555) 555-1234
wandaWB@email.com

How to Interview

Don't worry if you have to send out a few of these query letters to get a response; some people may simply be too busy to respond. When you do get someone who agrees to do an interview with you, have specific questions written down so you don't just end up babbling, respect the time limits you have set, and be sure to thank them for their time.

Have a pen and paper to make notes, or a tape recorder (ask permission to record them first), as this is great research for your business plan. You'll have a sense by the end of the interview as to whether or not this person may be open to mentoring you, or if you are uncertain, you can ask them outright. In order to get a positive response, make it clear that you don't plan to take up too much of their time. Set a guideline, such as one phone call and one email per month.

One way to speed up the process is to offer to pay the spa professional for their time and advice. Money opens many doors! Of course, this is what a spa consultant does for a living, so read on to decide if hiring a consultant is right for you.

Hiring a Spa Consultant

If you are new to the spa industry, or feel you are in over your head starting this business, you will want to look into hiring a consultant who is an expert in spas to help you get started. A consultant, using their experience to guide you, could potentially return to you every penny they charge, in the form of future revenue generated by sound and savvy business decisions.

They will advise you on whether your unique concept is viable (something this book obviously can't do), if it fits with the demographics in your area, and if the space you've chosen and designed is going to make you money, or is set up in a way to fritter cash away. If experienced, the consultant will have other spas to compare your project to, and can help you come up with realistic numbers of what you can make, and what it might cost you.

TIP: According to spa consultancy firm Preston Inc., a spa con-
       sultant will cost you anywhere from $500 to $5,000 a day,
       depending on the project and their experience.

Be warned, though: hiring a consultant is not your ticket to sit back
and let someone else do the work. "Even if you retain a consultant,
you need to have some base knowledge," cautions Sylvia Sepielli, spa
consultant, "so you can accurately evaluate whether to accept the advice
of the consultant."

When you are interviewing consultants (and you should interview
several before you choose one), remember that you can afford to be
picky. You have to ask yourself, if this individual knows so much about
running a spa, why aren't they doing that now? Or if you are up for it,
ask the consultant for their answer. A good consultant will have one
ready.

While unscrupulousness is not always the case, go into any consulting arrangement with a reasonable amount of skepticism, and let them
prove why using their services will be worth their fee. Remember that
you can also look for mentors (who will advise you for free or a minimal charge) as opposed to hiring consultants. That way you will be
getting advice from people who are successful and working in the spa
industry right now.

You can also try to use your suppliers and vendors as "spa consultants". If they sell you equipment or products, they can help with laying out your spa, creating your treatments, training your staff,
developing your marketing plan, etc. It makes sense to tap into all
your resources, especially the free ones.

As another option, the SCORE Association (Service Corps Of Retired
Executives) is a nonprofit association comprised of 11,500 volunteer
business counselors throughout the U.S. and its territories. There are
389 SCORE chapters in urban, suburban and rural communities. SCORE
members are trained to serve as counselors advisors and mentors to
aspiring entrepreneurs and business owners.

These services are offered at no fee, as a community service. SCORE
was formed in 1964 and nearly 4.5 million Americans have utilized

SCORE services. You can call 1 (800) 634-0245 for a referral to the SCORE chapter nearest to you.

Not everyone needs a coach or a consultant. Evaluate what you know and don't know, and get help if you need it. Below are two spa consultants recommended by Jeremy McCarthy, contributing writer to this guide. Jeremy has been involved in the launch of many high-end and resort spas. There are also a number of spa consultants interviewed for and quoted in this guide. Bear in mind that nobody can determine the right consultant, if any, for you, except yourself.

Alexis Ufland

Company: Lexi Design (owner)

Location: New York, NY

Website: **www.lexidesign.com**

Phone: (646) 736-1777

About: Specializes in building day spas from conception to completion. McCarthy says: "Ufland recognizes the importance of following all the way through the project. Her job is not over until the spa is fully operational and the employees feel comfortable in their new surroundings."

Neil Ducoff

Company: Strategies Publishing Group (president)

Location: Centerbrook, CT

Website: **www.strategies.com**

Phone: 1-800-417-4848, ext. 118

About: McCarthy says: "Ducoff has been doing educating and consulting for the salon and spa industries for more than 20 years. He specializes in helping the independent owners develop a profitable spa or salon."

3. Planning Your Spa

Now the fun really starts. It's time to start conceptualizing your spa, planning all the details that will make it unique. It's time to start formulating a plan, gathering up all the bits and pieces from your mind and pulling them together.

Do you want to open a franchise spa, or go independent? Pregnancy spa, or mobile spa? Do you want to buy an established spa? Do you want to build from scratch, or lease a building? And what level of renovations will your design concept require? You will want to put your ideas down on paper before you spend a single penny.

3.1 Envisioning Your Spa

> "One thing that I love about my job is that I get to be creative. You need a creative flair to succeed in this industry, and I think most of us love to exercise our creativity."
>
> — *Jeremy McCarthy, Spa Director and contributing author*

In the spa business, we get to create beautiful environments and peaceful, relaxing settings, try to imagine every detail to create just the right ambience for our guests. Then once we are done creating, we step back and say, "Okay, come on in!" It's a truly rewarding experience.

Any business is a constant process of evolution, but the ideas and concepts that are laid during this planning process will comprise 90% of what your business will become. With this in mind, it is important to spend a significant amount of time developing the concept of your "sanctuary". Even two to three months is not an unreasonable amount of time to spend to conduct research, feel out your ideas and confirm that your vision speaks to your soul as well as others'.

3.1.1 Brainstorming Ideas

Getting to the point of opening your doors takes a fair bit of planning. You'll want to sit down for several brainstorming sessions as you map out your vision of your new spa. The list of questions starting on the next page is designed to help you do just that.

As you answer each question, think about the message you will convey to your guests with that aspect of your planning, and if it fits in with your overall vision for the spa. When you ask "Why?" you mean, "What benefit does it have for the spa-goer?" Jot down your ideas, then look at them as a whole to pull your concept together.

> TIP: If you plan on opening your spa with a partner, you should complete this exercise together. Don't worry if you have more than one answer for a question, even if you are unsure at this point which one will be your ultimate choice. You'll sort that out in your actual business plan.

Spa Planning Questionnaire

1. What type of spa will you open?

   _____

2. Who owns this spa? Do partners have unique roles that suit their talents?

   _____

   _____

   _____

3. Who will be involved in planning the spa?

   _____

   _____

4. What is the name of your spa?   _____

5. Where does that name come from? Who thought of it? Why is it a fit for your spa?

   _____

   _____

   _____

   _____

6. Approximately how many square feet is your spa?   _____

7. How many clients would you serve in a day?   _____

8. How many treatment rooms do you plan for?   _____

9. How many staff members will you employ?   _____

10. What is the price of the average treatment at   _____
    your spa?

11. What is unique about your spa?

_____

_____

_____

_____

12. Is there a theme? How is this theme expressed uniformly throughout the spa?

_____

_____

_____

13. What does your "average" client look like? Male or female? Interests? Income?

_____

_____

_____

_____

14. What are three words you would want clients to use to describe your spa?

_____

15. What is your spa definitely NOT?

_____

_____

16. Where is your spa (ideally) located?

_____

_____

17. What is the history of the location?

_____

_____

18. What is unique about the location?

_____

_____

19. What is convenient to the location?

_____

_____

20. What is near or around the location?

_____

_____

21. What are some words that reflect your spa's design?

_____

22. What colors does it use and why? What do those colors represent?

_____

_____

23. What is the internal flow of traffic like, and why?

_____

_____

24. What are the internal and external sources of light?

_____

_____

25. Describe the airflow and sources of air in the spa.

_____

_____

26. What view do your clients have from inside?

_____

_____

27. What can you hear and smell in the spa?

_____

_____

_____

28. What amenities (nice little "extras") do you offer?

_____

_____

_____

29. What is available to eat and drink and why?

_____

_____

_____

30. What type of robes and slippers do you offer and why?

_____

_____

_____

31. What amenities are in the changing rooms and why?

_____

_____

_____

32. Where do guests relax before and after their treatment and why?

_____

_____

_____

33. What treatments do you offer?

_____

_____

_____

_____

_____

_____

_____

_____

_____

_____

_____

_____

You will want to answer questions 34 through 38 for each treatment mentioned in question 33.

34. What is the history of this treatment?

_____

_____

35. What are the benefits of having this treatment?

_____

_____

36. Why do you do this treatment?

_____

_____

37. What techniques does this treatment use and why?

_____

_____

38. What products do you use in this treatment?

_____

_____

39. What product lines would best represent the theme/style of your spa?

_____

_____

40. Why do you use those products? Who chose these products and why?

_____

_____

41. Who made the products and why? What is their background?

_____

_____

42. What are the ingredients? What is the history of those ingredients? Where do the ingredients come from?

_____

_____

43. What ingredients are not there and why?

_____

_____

44. Will you sell these products to clients?

_____

_____

"Dream-board" Your Spa

After answering the questions above to define your spa concept, use a dream-boarding exercise to work on sharpening your visual understanding of the spa. You'll want to reserve a two-to-four-hour period to do this exercise.

You'll need scissors, a glue stick and a blank poster board. Stock up on a variety of magazines from the business, lifestyle, beauty, fashion and spa industries. Cut out words, images and phrases that represent what you see in your spa design, customer base and image. Sometimes what you have trouble putting into words will come more easily in pictures!

A Sample Planning Exercise

One of this guide's contributing authors, Kibibi Springs, launched her mobile spa service, Moodivations, in 2002. Before she went into business, she thought about many of the same questions we have listed here to sharpen the focus of her business. She explains some of the process below as an example to help you in your planning.

> My mobile spa business had an overlying theme of 'total wellness' from the day of its inception. Everything about our services and product lines we offer are based on providing our customers with physical relaxation, mental rejuvenation and spiritual uplifting.
>
> The name 'Moodivations' is a combination of the words 'mood' and 'motivation'. Though we could have chosen to name the company Spa at Home or Spa to Go, it was important to us to choose a name that meant something in regards to what we personally value in a spa experience.
>
> While developing my company concept I repeatedly visualized what our ideal customer looked like. I still do. In doing this I was able to discover not only the types of customers that currently patronized spa establishments, but those customers who have the potential to patronize, but didn't because there was no marketing focus on them.
>
> My company's signature colors are two complementary shades of blue because research on the psychology of color and marketing shows that the color blue is the color that the majority of the world population calls its favorite color. It represents trust. Since the company is mobile and requires entering people's personal space, it was important to develop a subconscious level of trust with customers from the time they first saw our name.
>
> I was inspired by a local spa that offered use of a dry heat sauna, fully stocked book shelf of self-help and new age titles, and tea and water that I could indulge in during my relaxation period. Therefore, all of Moodivations' services come with an affirmation card and small gift item for the customer to let them know we appreciate their business and to introduce them to our self-named home spa product line.

3.1.2   Initial Market Research

It's very important that you test your ideas for your spa concept in the real world. You want to learn what services clients are willing to pay for, where they are currently going for spa services (if at all) and where your competition is falling short.

"The top three reasons people visit spas are: I'm stressed, I'm ill or I'm tired. That's it. Make me feel better than I did when I walked in. But most spas can do that with a simple massage. You have to be unique," says John Uhrig, CEO of Monochrome Marketing Solutions.

Never approach market research half-heartedly, because this is the foundation for putting together a business plan. Your business plan, of course, is a determining factor in you getting bank funding and investors for your spa. You need money to open your spa — it's that simple!

Looking at Demographics

When we spoke with spa owners in researching this guide, the term "demographics" came up again and again. Demographics simply mean the characteristics of a particular segment of the population. Each spa owner said they thoroughly researched the demographics of the area where they were considering opening their spa.

Such details as how many professional women over 40 live within a 15-mile radius, or how many men frequented day spas last year in your area may be important in determine income levels and desire for specialized services in your region.

If you find that the segment of the population that you want to target isn't readily available in your area, you may need to either shift your focus to a different group, say from men to women, or from high-end to affordable. Or you can choose to open your spa in another area where your target consumer can be found in abundance. Either way, knowing where you stand is far better than building your business on guesses.

How to Get Information

Demographics information can be found in a variety of grassroots ways. For example, if you intend to cater to brides, a simple call to the courthouse in your area to ask how many marriage licenses were given out in a certain county or town over the last several years will tell you how many weddings are being planned yearly.

You can try contacting the community association in urban areas, as well as the office of the city or town itself. Most will have demographics figures that will help you in your research.

One marketing firm working for a start-up spa company told us they called or visited more than 50 spas in the area their client was planning to open. The firm posed as potential clients wanting information about each spa. They asked questions like, "What is your area of expertise?" and "What service do most people get when they visit the first time?" If you have a few dedicated friends and some time, you can enlist their help and do this research yourself.

John Uhrig, CEO of Monochrome Marketing Solutions, suggests getting out on the streets where the potential customers are and asking them what they want in a spa. His company sets up survey stands in local malls, at trade shows, spa events and association luncheons. They ask questions like:

- Have you ever visited a spa?

- How often do you visit spas?

- What did you like about the spa?

- What didn't you like?

"You have to look at marketing like building a case in court. The more you've researched and the more compelling your evidence, the more assured you are of getting the results that you want," says Uhrig.

Using Research Professionals

A faster and easier (but more expensive) way to get the information you need is to hire a marketing firm. With the spa industry growing at such a rapid rate, there are firms that work extensively in the spa industry, as well as individual consultants as discussed earlier. Whether or not you use a marketing firm or consultant to do your initial market research really depends on which you have more of: time, or money.

Two spa-focused marketing firms you can contact are Monochrome Marketing Solutions, Inc. at **www.spamarketing.ca** and Day Spa Marketing at **www.dayspamarketing.com**. Or simply type "spa" and "marketing" or "consulting" into your favorite search engine.

3.1.3 Choosing a Niche

Once you know what the market in the location for your spa is like, and you know what the competition is offering, you are ready to match that information with a niche for your spa. A niche is simply an area where you stand out — something unique from the rest.

"Initially, day spas tried to be everything to everybody. Anything that was spa-oriented was stuffed into a 2,000 square-foot space with a fifteen-page menu of service and sometimes up to 65 different facials," explains spa consultant Alexis Ufland, in an article posted on the About. com website. "The result was that everything fought each other and nothing was profitable. Today, you will see spas that specialize; they do one thing and they do it well." You can read the whole article, which is full of excellent advice, at **http://spas.about.com/od/medispas**

Determining a niche for your spa comes from a combination of what isn't offered by the competition, and what is important to you. Most spa owners admit that their niche grew out of their personal passion and beliefs.

Stephanie Palko, owner of Copperfalls Aveda Day Spa in Castle Rock, Colorado, says, "You have to ask yourself what it is that will make your spa different and enticing to a potential customer. Ours is the product line we choose to align ourselves with. I've always been interested in essential oils and natural healing, so Aveda is aligned with my beliefs."

Terri Malueg-Ray, owner of Royal Paws Resort & Day Spa, advises to follow your heart, even when it leads to unconventional places. "When I started my spa for pets, people thought it was a joke. I love my dog. When he developed arthritis, I researched natural ways to help him. I found it through massage, and thought other people should know about the health benefits in pet massages. The business grew out of my love for pets."

Niche Ideas to Consider

Whatever your passion, be it gourmet food, technology, animals, Eastern philosophy, or fitness, you can find a way to integrate it into your spa. Some niche spas that are popular right now focus on the following unique features. What type of spa do you see yourself running?

Unique Clientele

- Pregnancy spas, where services are catered to expectant moms

- Family spas, which provide babysitting and/or a kid-friendly environment

- Men's spas, where services are geared towards a man's sensibility

- Couple spas, which provide an environment conducive to human bonding between husbands and wives, mothers and daughters, or close friends

Unique Location

- Nature spas, where treatments are conducted outdoors in a breathtaking setting

- Mobile or portable spas, which bring spa services into clients' homes or offices

Unique Services

- Medical or dental spas, where spa services are paired with medical and dental treatments*

- Cosmetic spas, which combine traditional spa treatments with anti-aging treatments such as Botox and chemical peels*

* *Spas offering medical services require additional licensing or staff members with accreditation, and may require that a doctor or nurse is onsite. You will want to research thoroughly with a consultant and contact all necessary licensing agencies before deciding on this niche.*

- Educational or self-help spas, which feature classes and seminars on services that can be recreated at home such as makeup application, facials and foot treatments

- Express spas, which specialize in mini-services (15-30 minutes) for customers on the go

- Nail spas, which focus exclusively on the hands and feet

- Luxury spas, which specialize in little extras such as complimentary massages, makeup application, or take-home robes and slippers

Note that you don't have to limit yourself to one niche, but can combine them for a unique approach. As contributing author Kibibi Springs explains, "I used 11 unique concepts when building my mobile spa business, and there's always room for additional conceptual growth." That said, you don't want to market your spa to "everyone," so make sure that you have reasonable focus.

Another pitfall to avoid is getting caught up in fashionable trends that are not going to last. This doesn't mean that you should be afraid to do something that has never been done before. It could be the key to your success. But don't choose a niche because it is fashionable — choose it because it is sound and viable.

3.2   Business Options

> "My business partner and I chose a mobile business model because we didn't want to be committed to a specific location and its overhead. At this point in our lives, we appreciate the flexibility that a mobile business offers."
>
> — *Kibibi Springs, spa owner, Moodivations*

Today there are more options than ever to develop a spa business. The decision of which direction you choose will depend greatly on the amount of capital you have at your access or are able to raise, as well as your personal preferences. Here are some of the options you can consider for opening your spa.

3.2.1 A Brand New Spa

The most traditional spa business is a "brick and mortar" establishment, and can range from an elaborately decorated stand-alone spa, to a smaller local or strip mall day spa. Since you are starting fresh you will need to find and renovate a location, purchase all equipment and supplies, hire a full staff and develop a client base.

You may purchase land and build a facility from the ground up, or buy or rent a space and transform it into your spa facility. Building from scratch allows total creative freedom for design, and although it may seem like an odd advantage, the building time allows plenty of opportunity for pre-publicity with the neighborhood and local street traffic.

The drawback is of course the cost, since your expenses to get an average day spa up and running will likely range from $250,000 to $500,000 just to open your doors. Your biggest cost likely will be your building and renovations, followed closely by the equipment, furnishings, and supplies.

A drawback to this business option is the uncertainty. Construction tends to have an unreliable time frame, meaning that you can't count on a certain day to start your business. There are too many variables to be certain until the last minute exactly what your timeline and total costs will be to renovate.

Details to Consider

If you are planning to purchase a building or land and build or renovate your spa, your primary consideration is going to be the location. You will have total freedom (within reason) to purchase wherever you think is going to best suit your needs. Section 4.1 goes into details on the nuances of selecting a location for your spa, such as neighborhood, parking, walk-by traffic, etc.

Another consideration is whether to lease a building or buy your space, and this comes down to how much money you have available. Tom Hennessy, author of *FabJob Guide to Become a Restaurant Owner* and *FabJob Guide to Become a Coffee House Owner* (two other "fab" businesses to start), offers the following advice on this great debate:

If you have the money, I think buying is the way to go. I still kick myself when I think about the chance we had to buy our building in one of our restaurants. We had been in business for about a year and it was going well. The landlord offered to sell us our section of the building, which included our space plus three more commercial spaces for $250,000.

This was back in 1989 and that seemed like a lot of money, so we didn't do it. We never even took the time to calculate the monthly payment, which would have been minimal. The restaurant is still in business and is approaching the $2-million mark in rents paid. Ouch!

When you own your own building, all the building or improvements you will be doing will be going into something you own, thereby increasing the value of your asset. Plus you may find that your monthly payment might not be any different than the rent you would be paying.

If you are in the position to buy the location, talk to your lawyer and accountant about this. They may recommend that you create a separate company to own the building and lease it out to yourself. It makes a lot of sense tax-wise to do this. If the building is of historic value, it may also be eligible for low-interest improvement loans.

If you cannot afford the building or it is not for sale, you may be able to negotiate a first right of refusal into your lease, whereby if the building ever comes up for sale in the future, you have the first right to purchase it.

If you do decide to lease the building, you have the right to ask the landlord to contribute some money for a portion of the improvement costs. They are not always opposed to this because it improves their building.

At a minimum, it never hurts to ask the landlord not to charge you rent while you are under construction. If on the other hand, you are getting a great location for a tiny amount of rent, you may not get any concessions from the landlord.

Chapter 5 of this guide will explain many more of the details you'll want to handle before signing a lease or purchase agreement, including spa-specific engineering inspections, and making sure the building will suit your needs.

Consider Existing Spaces

One way to potentially save time and money is to initiate a business partnership with an existing business such as a fitness center, hotel or coffee shop to include a spa facility in their business expansion plans. The contract time could be cut in half, and you have a built-in customer base that you can piggy back on, reliable and measurable foot traffic, and built-in cross-marketing opportunities.

Of course partnering is not without its challenges, either. The existing business model and staff may not accommodate your style of doing business, or they may require more compromises on aesthetic ideas than you'd like. Most businesses will also expect a split of your profits to accommodate you.

You may find better luck approaching local non-chain businesses than the downtown Sheraton Hotel. The fancy hotels have a national reputation to uphold, and taking a risk on a new or inexperienced spa owner is not something they'll take lightly. This may be a direction you can grow towards, though, down the road when you are established and successful.

3.2.2   Buy an Existing Spa

Purchasing an existing spa can provide a shortcut to your opening day and allow you the ease of slipping into a situation that is already profitable with potential for growth. Since renovations will be a major cost factor, if you can stumble upon a place for sale that is already set up with reception, treatment rooms, showers, etc. you are saving yourself considerable money. Even if you plan a remodel, it is a lot simpler than building from scratch.

Rather than spending $500,000 or more on your build-out and equipment for a day spa, you are likely to find existing spas for sale in the range of $75,000 to $250,000. Of course, if you are looking at purchasing a resort spa in the Caribbean, you are looking in the millions of dollars instead! Be warned, though: purchasing an existing spa does not guarantee you will walk into an arrangement that meets your "ready for business" criteria.

Remember the 2005 movie *Beauty Shop* starring Queen Latifah? Frustrated with a lack of respect from her boss, Latifah's character Gina purchases a run-down salon to open her own business. Getting the space into working condition was not without its challenges, and your adventures may be just as challenging.

Details to Consider

If you make what's called a stock purchase, it means you are buying everything, from inventory to liabilities. You will be responsible for any debts the spa has incurred. If you make what's called an asset purchase, you will only be buying the material part of the spa, and the previous owner will be responsible for any outstanding financial matters. This is a crucial difference to keep in mind.

If you are buying a spa that is still in business, most owners selling will be willing to train you on the details of the operation, and may also be available to assist you on a consulting basis for the first six months to a year of your ownership. You should also expect owners to sign a non-competing clause that assures you they will not start up another spa nearby once they've sold the old one to you.

> **TIP:** When interviewing the current owner during negotiations to buy an existing spa business, be sure to ask to see the sales reports from at least the last year, and preferably the last few years. Knowing if the business suffers from any seasonal sales slumps (and most businesses do) will help you to prepare and plan your annual sales goals.

Always inquire about the details of the current lease — what your lease renewal options are, and anything specific to the uses of the area immediately outside and in back of your establishment. You'll want to know if you have exclusivity rights within the location/area if you are in a mall or strip mall.

You stand to benefit from a position of easier growth for your spa with existing customers, depending on the previous owner's marketing savvy and personal effort level, and employees. This is a double-edged sword, though — if the business was run poorly, past clients will associate you with the same level of service. If this is the case, you will want to make sure the public can tell you are a new, unaffiliated spa.

Existing employees who transfer to working for you can also be either a positive or a negative factor. If you plan to overhaul not just the façade of the establishment, but also how the business is run, existing employees will need to get on board with the new program. Good employees will bring with them loyal clients, which can help you as an owner.

If you want to keep the spa's same name and branding, the previous owners may request a percentage of your profits. As spas often operate on a thin profit margin, this seemingly small amount may cut into your cash flow in a serious way. Think carefully before you agree to any such terms. If the existing business model and staff don't accommodate your style of doing business or require more compromise on aesthetic ideas than you'd prefer, you'll want to plan a total overhaul anyway.

Where to Find Spas for Sale

Here are some websites where you can find existing spa businesses for sale. You can also search your local newspapers if you don't want to change locations, or even approach spa owners directly. Everyone has a price!

- *Business Nation: Businesses for Sale*
  **www.businessnation.com/Businesses_for_Sale/
  General_Service/Salons/Massage-Spas/**

- *BizBuySell*
  www.bizbuysell.com/beauty-and-barber-shops-for-sale

- *Businesses for Sale.com*
  www.businessesforsale.com/

3.2.3   A Franchise Spa

If you are eager to open your own spa, but are concerned about how much work is involved in getting everything set up, or are concerned about the riskiness of an untested business venture, you may want to consider franchising.

Franchising happens when an established company allows someone to run a local business using its company name, logo, products, services, marketing, and business systems. The original company is known as the "franchisor", and the company that is granted the right to run its business is known as the "franchisee".

Deciding if a Franchise Suits You

People who choose to franchise rather than start their own spa from scratch often do so because they want to minimize their risk. They see the franchise as a proven business that already has name recognition among the public. By working with an established system, franchisees hope to avoid costly mistakes and make a profit more quickly.

Franchises are also good for people who have less business know-how, and want support. Franchisors typically provide training to help franchisees start, market and run their new business. The franchisee may receive assistance in everything from obtaining supplies to setting up record-keeping systems. Many franchisors are continuously working to develop better systems and products, and franchisees can take advantage of these developments. Some provide comprehensive training and related products for you to sell.

It is important to keep in mind that a franchisee does not own any of the company's trademarks or business systems. Also, a franchisee must run his or her business according to the terms of the agreement with the franchisor. For example, the franchisee may not be permitted to offer a sales promotion or use a supplier that has not been authorized by the franchisor.

While some people appreciate having such guidelines to follow, if you are an independent person who enjoys taking risks and being spontaneous, you might find owning a franchise to be too restrictive. Since someone else is ultimately in charge, you may be wondering how having a franchise is different from managing someone else's spa. In fact, there are significant differences. You have more freedom that an employee would (you might choose your own working hours, for example). And you could ultimately earn much more money than an employee.

Although the franchise itself may be quite successful, there is no guarantee that you will be successful after linking up with them and doing business. You may not get the support you had hoped for from the franchisor, or you might find that the geographic location is not right for the business.

TIP: What you receive for your investment varies from franchise to franchise, so make sure you know exactly what you will be buying, since franchising is a long-term relationship. You may want to hire a franchise consultant, or consult with your lawyer and accountant before you sign a franchise contract. You can learn about options for free consultation at the Franchise Consultation website at **www.franchise-consultation.com**.

Franchise Costs

On average, a franchise is going to cost you more to start up than an independent spa, but you are gambling on it helping you make a faster profit. Spa franchises on average require a minimum investment of $250,000, an average of about $500,000, and for big names, gets into the $1 million-plus range. The initial investment typically includes two components: the payment of a franchise fee, and the balance to cover your start-up costs.

For example, Yevgeniya's Russian Day Spa is a Colorado-based spa franchise that caters to both male and female spa clients. Its franchise fee is $10,000. Their website (**www.russiandayspa.com/dayspafranchise. html**) estimates initial investment costs, including items such as a grand opening, leasehold improvements, equipment, inventory, insurance, etc., at $137,000-$271,000.

In addition to your initial investment, you can expect to pay the franchisor ongoing royalties, which typically range from 7 to 11 per-cent of your sales; the exact amount will be determined by the company you franchise with.

Finding a Franchise

There aren't a ton of spa franchises open for the public to start up, and it seems that many specialize in medical services. Here are a few for a quick example. Note that the companies listed here are provided as examples only, and are not endorsed or recommended. Only you can decide which franchise, if any, is right for you.

- *Woodhouse Spas*
  www.woodhousefranchises.com/investmentcosts.asp

- *Jonric International*
  www.jonric.com/franchise_opportunities.htm

- *Radiance Medspa*
  www.radiancefranchise.com/franchise_opportunity.php

For a more comprehensive list, visit the International Franchise Association's website, and search on the term "spa."

- *Franchise Opportunities*
  www.franchise.org

3.2.4 A Spa/Salon

The advantages of offering salon services at your spa are great. First, your clients will appreciate that they can combine all their beauty treatments into one session, instead of getting a facial at one place, and a haircut at another. The advantage to you as spa owner is the chance to up-sell clients on your many services each time they book with you.

Another benefit to the spa/salon owner is that salon services are usually sought out more frequently than spa services. Your salon clients end up coming in more frequently, which is a reminder to them that they may require a spa treatment as well. Combining these services encourages clients to regard their spa treatments as "required maintenance" as opposed to a luxury.

An additional incentive to offering spa/salon services is that it allows you to offer more complete pampering packages to key markets like bridal parties. The clients can come in and benefit from the relaxing and rejuvenating benefits of a spa treatment, and then round out their day with hair and makeup so they can walk out feeling truly great about themselves. It also helps you offer a more attractive package for corporate or family bookings, and gift certificate purchases.

Perhaps the most attractive aspect of combining spa and salon services is the opportunity to service more clients, and therefore make more money. Salons generally run at a slightly higher profit margin than spas, so the chance to recoup some of your start-up expenses more quickly than if you offer spa services alone is appealing to many would-be day spa owners.

So with all the obvious benefits of offering combined spa/salon services, why is it that not all spas offer haircutting, and not all salons offer massages? One of the primary concerns is the very different nature of salon and spa services.

Spa services are almost always offered in a private, dimly lit, tranquil environment. There may be little or no communication between the service provider and the recipient. Salon service, on the other hand, tends to be conducted in well-lit semi-private or public settings. Hairdryers are blasting, the radio may be jangling a tune, and each station is buzzing with its own chit-chat between stylist and client.

As a spa/salon owner, these diverse elements can be tough to manage exclusively, as they require specific layout and additional square footage. Ideally, a spa/salon should be designed and planned as such, since integrating them as an afterthought can be both challenging and expensive.

When you are planning the layout of your space, take a look at where the spa and salon services will be offered. In some cases spa/salons will have the spa on one level of the building, and the salon on another. Note that the salon is a better match with the entrance, reception, lockers, etc., while the spa services should be offered in the area of greatest privacy. Think hard about how noise is likely to travel from one area to the other. You may even want to have a separate check-in for your spa.

Recently, many salons have looked to capitalize on the success of the day spa by adding spa services. Salon owners looking to add spa services to their menu should be aware that they will need additional, private rooms, and if they want to offer wet treatments or shower facilities, plumbing and drainage may be an issue. You'll also need to factor in additional equipment and supplies.

Since design and ambiance are more of a factor in a spa versus a salon, renovations in the range of $100,000 to $200,000 are not unheard of in this instance. Before deciding to expand to a spa/salon, make sure that there is a market for spa services with your existing clientele, and in the surrounding market.

Alternately, spa owners who want to offer hair and nail services should be aware that there can be a stigma attached to calling yourself a spa/salon. Some salons have tried to cheaply capitalize on the spa trend by adding "and day spa" onto the end of their name, but in actuality offering limited services in an imperfect environment.

For this reason, many day spas (especially ones not associated with resorts or hotels) actually do not offer salon services. If you plan on marketing your stand-alone spa to primarily upscale clients, you may want to consider advertising your salon services as a simple bonus to your service menu, as opposed to tacking it onto your moniker. Alternately, for a true salon/spa in something like a mall location, a salon/spa combo name could be an absolute benefit, so consider your target market.

Also, since salon and spa treatment providers require very different training, you'll need to hire separate staff, and possibly separate managers, for these two domains. If you are personally unfamiliar with one element of the service (spa or salon), make sure that the people you bring in are experienced and knowledgeable in their specialty. Of course, it's also great if a stylist can bring his or her loyal clients along too!

In some cases, independent contractors are brought in to provide additional services for a flat fee, to avoid adding to staffing budgets. This makes the most sense if your main goal is to add complementary services and increase traffic, though — not if you are looking to make money off the new service.

3.2.5   A Mobile Spa Service

This exciting new trend in spas is opening the doors to individuals who want to start a business to offer spa services, but also need to minimize their start-up costs. Mobile spa businesses do not have a "brick-and-mortar" location where clients come, but instead bring spa services directly to the home or office.

You will still need to purchase supplies and materials to conduct spa parties, get required business licenses, hire and train staff, and create and distribute marketing materials, but not having to renovate and pay rent or a mortgage on a physical space makes this a much more economical start-up option.

According to Kibibi Springs, a contributing author who opened her own mobile spa business in 2002, you should expect to spend between $1,500 and $4,000 to start up a very basic mobile spa service. One extra expense you may encounter would be the purchase or lease of company vehicles for your technicians, if you do not have these available.

As a new industry option, it also means there is tons of potential for growth if you are one of the first in your market to introduce the service. This can be an initial challenge as you may have to work harder to sell the idea to clients, but the potential benefits are there for mobile spas that are successful in the long run.

If you are unsure where to start, there are many companies that offer business opportunities in the mobile spa business. They will provide you with a training manual that outlines the details for running your business, marketing supplies and guidelines for securing professionals to provide services. In some cases you will also buy the rights to use their name and branding locally. Here are some companies that offer mobile spa consultation and business opportunities.

- *MobileSpa*
  www.mobilespa.com/busi.asp

- *Mobile Day Spa*
  **www.mobilehomespa.com/
  Mobile_Day_Spa_Business_Opportunity.html**

- *Moodivations*
  www.moodivations.com

3.3 Your Business Plan

This section of the guide was written with the help of spa business owner and contributing author Kibibi Springs, *who has kindly shared portions of her business plan for her spa company Moodivations. Proprietary information specific to the details of the business has been omitted.*

Your business plan is your road map to success, and you will need one to start your spa. Before you panic, understand that a business plan does not have to be a 60-page document with complex charts and graphs to impress business partners and banks. In fact, often the simpler your plan is, the better. The point is to get across what makes your business tick, why it's a fantastic idea and why people should want to get on board.

3.3.1 Do I Need a Business Plan?

Even if you don't plan to approach a bank to open your spa, a business plan is still very important. You will also use your plan to communicate your unique vision of your spa to contractors you hire to build and design your spa, and to education your staff and/or manager or director about what you are trying to accomplish. You may have a perfect vision of what you want in your head, but if you don't put it down on paper for others to see, you risk serious miscommunication that could be costly – or "fatal" – to your spa.

Writing your business plan does a couple of things. It:

- Defines your spa project, both for you and for potential investors

- Measures the feasibility of the project, and projects the profit you expect

- Shows you are organized and have done the necessary research

- Shows your vendors, architects, designers and contractors the "larger vision"

The business plan can start off as a general idea, a direction you want to head in, the concepts and ideas your business will be based on. Be as specific as you can while leaving room for changes as your spa comes to life.

"Even with a college degree and 10 years in strategic planning positions within corporate America, I was challenged by the development of my business plan. I did massive research, interviewed people and bought about ten books on the subject before I came across one that made a light bulb go off in my head," says Kibibi Springs. That book was *Successful Business Models*, by Don Debelak (part of the *Entrepreneur Mentor Series*).

It is important to note that a business plan is an evolving document. Though the concept and foundation of the business may stay the same, the marketing, operations and financials evolve as you learn more about how your business grows, makes money and services for the clients it was intended.

3.3.2   Parts of the Plan

Now, let's walk through each section of your business plan and how it should be written.

The Executive Summary

The most frequently read piece of your business plan will be the executive summary. It gives potential investors a "snapshot" or concise overview of your idea and why it's a money maker, and is an enticement to read the rest of your plan.

The executive summary is no more than five (and most often, two or three) pages of overview on the key elements of your business. Your summary should include all the same elements of your business plan listed below, summarized into concise paragraphs. Then the complete business plan is an elaboration on each of those sections with additional detail and your complete set of financials.

"It needs to entice the reader," says spa consultant Alexis Ufland. "The first page [your executive summary] determines whether or not they read the rest of the plan."

> TIP: You don't really need to sit down and "write" an executive summary. Write the rest of your business plan first, and then use a highlighter to go through and pick out the key points. When you make your summary, you can "cut and paste" directly from the rest of the plan.

Company Description

In a concise page to page and a half, explain your business. What are you called, what do you sell or do, and what makes you unique? You can break this section down into the nature of the business (two paragraphs on the market niche your company will fill), and unique competencies (why your location and plan is perfect). Here is the type of language you will use in this section:

"Moodivations is a total-wellness company that offers stress-relief and stress-management through a unique in-home and office spa service and three branded product lines."

Market Analysis

This section offers you the opportunity to show the reader how much you already know about your industry. You'll want to highlight where the industry currently stands on total annual revenues and significant trends which support your business model.

This is also the section where you whip out those mind-boggling statistics and demographics that scream out, "This idea is a WINNER!" Don't rely on assumptions; instead, cite the most reliable sources of data you have access to (see the previous section 3.1.2 for tips on building a case of market research). Professional associations like the ISPA are also good sources of convincing data on the spa industry. You can use it to craft catchy paragraphs like the following:

"Stimulated by an increased interest in health and fitness, a day at the spa has become one of the most sophisticated and exciting ways of vacationing and spending discretionary income in the 21st century. Whether the customer is seeking an escape from work-related stress or to engage in a bit of self-indulgence, there are a variety of spa experiences to choose from, making the industry ripe for new concepts and niche markets."

Customer

Now is when you show the reader that you know your customer — what they look like, live like and most importantly, BUY like. Include specific details regarding their demographics such as age, ethnicity, gender, geographic locations, and socioeconomic status (annual income, spending habits, and lifestyle patterns). If you have more than one target customer, explain the unique features of each. For example:

"Our first target customer is a current 'Spa-Goer'. We see this customer as an active, health-conscious woman between the ages of 16 and 45 who embraces traditional spa activity and seeks new ways to alleviate stress and incorporate more relaxation and reflection into her lifestyle..."

Competitive Strategy

Potential investors will zone in on this particular section of your plan, because it tells them what makes you different from your competition. (It's also one of the sections where we cannot give you a direct example from Moodivations' business plan, because it is the core of how any business intends to out-do their competition!) Your competitive strategy should focus on the following:

- Is your pricing higher or lower than your competitors, and why?

- What features are highlighted in your business (speed, convenience, service)?

Marketing Strategy

Your marketing strategy focuses on how you intend to reach your target customer. Again, you want to show that you've done your homework on your customer and pull out the most important details that illustrate this. Your marketing strategy should answer the following questions:

- How will you approach your customer?

- What channels and mediums will you use to speak to them?

- Is there anything about your pricing that benefits your marketing strategy?

- What markets/industries will you use to reach your target customer?

- Will you be targeting any customers that are currently not being addressed in your industry, and why?

Sales Strategy

This section specifies how you intend to achieve your company's monetary goals. The executive summary includes two to five sentences about your sales strategy, while the full business plan goes into the details of how you plan to execute that strategy with your employee/sales team(s).

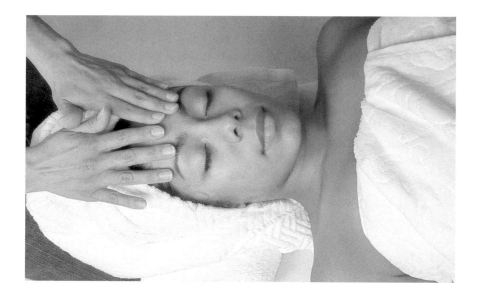

"Moodivations will direct its sales team to aim for 'x' % of the discretionary income currently being spent in the spa and beauty industry. We calculate a minimum of 'x' reservations per month and product and service sales of 'x' per month to achieve this goal."

Projected Goal

This section should capture an overview of financial objectives for your business within a stated time frame. This section can often be confused with the sales strategy. The slight difference is your goal states the overall monetary goal for the company, whereas, the sales strategy is a breakdown of how you will direct your sales team(s) to achieve that goal.

"Moodivations' overall goal is to acquire (this percentage) of the combined revenues (note amount) shared between its common industries (named here) in the next 3 to 5 years. Moodivations will execute a company launch, staffing, marketing and sales activity to reach revenues of (this amount) by (this date)."

Services and Products

In this section, go into depth about what it is that you sell. Highlight any distinguishing features that set you apart from similar products or services in your industry. You might explain any copyrights, patents or trade secrets you have for spa services or products you have developed.

> "Moodivations offers the enjoyments of a day spa within the comforts of home. Our service offerings include five spa experiences and six Signature Treatments, which include A, B, C, D, E, and F ..."

Operations

Explain in this section how you will deliver spa services and products to your client. Detail the square footage of your spa, your hours of operation, your number of employees, the number of treatment rooms and types of treatments you will offer, and any plans for future expansion. If you have them (and it will look far more professional if you do), you can also include:

- Your operations manual and/or employee manual
- Your planned starting inventory of product
- A detailed list of the equipment you'll use
- Your roughed out menu of services

Management and Ownership

Here is where you explain how the ownership of the company is divided (if at all) and the backgrounds of the owners as they relate to the potential success of the business.

> "Moodivations is a four-year-old privately owned company based in Sherman Oaks, California. It is equally owned by creative partners Alicia Jackson and Kibibi Springs.
>
> Kibibi Springs brings 10 years of public relations, marketing and business development talent to the company. With 10 years of consumer PR experience, Kibibi has spent most of her career in the beauty industry, etc. ..."

Financial Data

If you are seeking funding, your business plan should conclude with a statement of the total dollar amount you want to borrow, both immediately and over the next five years. It should also state what you plan to use those funds for, and outline your long-term financial strategies that may require more funding down the road (expansion of your spa, building another location, etc.).

Your business plan will conclude with projected financial statements that are more detailed for the first year, and have less specific information up to year 3 or 5. These financial documents provide evidence that you have thought your plan through, accounted for all expenses, and most importantly to banks and investors, that you have a solid process in place to pay back lenders. You will also include some details of assumptions you have based your calculations on, since nobody knows exactly what the future will bring in terms of economy and other factors.

You may need to provide what is called a break-even analysis, which shows how much income it will take just to cover your expenses, or the point at which you start being able to keep some of the money you make. In a spa setting, this may be calculated in number of clients per month, based on an average price per client, and may or may not include product sales.

Many people erroneously assume that the spa will start putting money in their pockets immediately, but because there is such a huge output of spending at the beginning, it can take several years to get rolling. Sections 3.4 and 5.5 have more information on planning a startup and operational budget for your spa.

"If you do not feel comfortable outlining your own financials, I suggest you bring in a professional to detail this information for you. A bookkeeper or accountant could be helpful, but costly," advises Kibibi. She adds, "Another route which has benefited many of the entrepreneurs I know is to enlist the help of an MBA student. MBA students learn all the basics regarding business plan development in their curriculum, and for a small fee, an MBA student would be more than willing to test their new skill set with a new variety of business model."

Financial Projection

On the facing page is a simple version of a complete financial chart to illustrate how financials are mapped out from quarter-to-quarter and how increases in sales projections increase the bottom line. It does not include all possible expenses (rent, housekeeping, etc.) in order to simplify it for educational purposes. Detailed information on startup- cost-estimating can be found in the following section of the guide.

Sample Financial Projection

	Average Sale Per Customer	# Services/Sales per month x # Techs	1st Quarter	# Services per month x # Techs	2nd Quarter
Revenue					
Massage Services	$100	30(3)	$27,000	50(3)	$45,000
Esthetician Services	$95	20(2)	$11,000	30(2)	$17,100
Manicure Services	$35	40(2)	$8,400	50(3)	$15,750
Product Sales	$40	50	$6,000	70	$8,400
Total Revenue			$52,400		$86,250
Total Cost of Goods (40% of product sales)			$2,400		$3,360
Salaries (30% of service revenue)			$13,920		$23,355
Gross Profit			$36,080		$59,535
Operating Expenses					
Owner Salary			$10,000		$10,000
Receptionist Salary @ $10/ hour 60 hr week			$7,800		$7,800
Equipment Leases			$6,000		$6,000
Bookkeeper/Accounting			$1,500		$1,500
Liability Insurance			$3,000		$3,000
Marketing Expenses			$3,000		$3,000
Supplies			$3,000		$3,000
Misc./Petty Cash			$900		$900
Total Expenses			$35,200		$35,200
Net Operating Income (Gross Profit – Total Expenses)			$880		$24,335

Other Parts of Your Plan

Your plan should also include the following extra material and information:

- A cover sheet. This identifies your business and explains the purpose of the business plan. Be sure to include your name, the name of the business and any partners you might have, your address, phone number, email and other pertinent information. You can also note that your plan is confidential and should not be copied.

- Table of contents. This goes just under your cover sheet and tells what is included in your business plan. Use major headings and subheadings to identify content.

- Supporting documents. Include your personal (and business, if applicable) tax returns for the past three years, a personal financial statement (get a form from your bank) and a copy of a lease or purchase agreement if you're going to be buying or renting office space. You can also include your resume, and any related marketing materials you've already prepared for the spa.

3.3.3   Business Plan Help

Many entrepreneurs use the United States Small Business Administration (SBA)'s business plan outline as a model when writing this document. The Canada Business Service Centres (CBSC) also provides a sample business plan, and American Express offers a user-friendly guide as well.

- *SBA: Business Plan Basics*
  www.sba.gov/smallbusinessplanner/plan/writeabusinessplan

- *CBSC: Business Start-up Assistant*
  http://bsa.canadabusiness.ca

- *Creating an Effective Business Plan*
  http://www133.americanexpress.com/osbn/tool/biz_plan/

As mentioned earlier, the Service Corps Of Retired Executives has volunteers throughout the U.S. who donate time to mentor small businesses free of charge. Their site at **www.score.org** also has helpful articles.

The Business Development Bank of Canada (BDC) offer good advice as well as free business plan samples and templates at **www.bdc.ca/en/ business_tools/business_plan**.

3.4   Start-Up Costs & Funding

A key component of your business plan will be determining how much money you'll need to start your business. This can vary wildly depending on contractors' fees, extravagance of the design, your proposed location and whether you plan to rent or buy, among other things.

3.4.1 Your Start-Up Expenses

Generally, the top three start-up costs assuming you do not purchase a building would-be spa owners will encounter and their approximate percentage of start-up expense are:

- Construction/renovation and decorating (25 - 35% or more)

- Furniture and equipment (15% - 20% or more)

- Initial inventory and supplies (8 - 10%)

If you do plan to buy the building, factor in a down payment on the mortgage into your major costs as well. Check with a mortgage broker to get an idea of what this amount is likely to be based on the asking price.

Construction/Renovation and Decorating

This will cover the cost of design, materials, and labor to convert an existing facility into a spa — to build from ground up will be even higher. While an estimate of 25 to 35 percent of your total cost may seem high, you have to take into account everything from having the building inspected to your architectural costs (these professionals charge hundreds of dollars an hour) to building permits, to materials, contractor fees, decoration consulting, and so on. A complex or luxury renovation can run you up to 50% of your start-up cost, or more.

A spa is not a simple commercial renovation (not that such a thing really exists!) — since you are dividing the space into numerous rooms, there are complex plumbing issues, etc. And since people are coming for a luxury service, decorating has to be top-notch or you'll look no more appealing than the doctor's office. Even the cost of outdoor and indoor signage can be significant. If you are opening a mobile spa then of course you will save on many or all of these costs.

Furniture and Equipment

This estimate of 15 to 20 percent covers basic equipment like your treatment beds or chairs, facial equipment, relaxation lounge furniture, front desk, computer, sound system and so on. If you do laundry on-site, commercial washers and dryers are needed. You may or may not realize that even a low-end chair for esthetic services can cost you $1,000!

This percentage accounts for only the basics, and there is a lot of high-end spa equipment you can add that would drive the initial cost up. More details on the equipment and supplies you will need (or may desire) can be found in section 4.3.

Initial Inventory and Supplies

This cost includes both the products you'll sell and the products and small items you'll use on a daily basis in your treatment rooms, office, etc. Whether or not you pay for the items you sell up front would have to be worked out with your vendor, but your treatment supplies have to be in place before you book your first client. This may also include staff uniforms, towels, and other items that, while reusable, still need to be purchased (and replaced when worn out).

Other Start-Up Costs

Here is a list of other expenses you may encounter in setting up your spa. You will not necessarily have to put money out on all of these, but don't overlook the possibility. In the next section on budgeting, we'll plug in some numbers so you can see how they balance out:

- Insurance
- Spa consultant
- Deposit on lease/down-payment on mortgage
- Professional fees (lawyer, accountant, marketing, etc.)
- Marketing/advertising
- Pre-opening staff training
- Graphic design/website design
- Printing (menus, stationery)
- Computer software
- Business licenses and permits

- Voluntary accreditation
- Professional memberships
- Deposit on utilities and phone

The Importance of a "Nest Egg"

You will need money to build or buy your spa, but once it is ready, don't forget to have money in the bank to pay the expenses and keep it running. This is called working capital, and is an often overlooked expense you need to plan for.

Depending on the type and style of spa, this may add up to 5 to 15 percent of your total start-up budget, although some experts suggest you could simply have credit available instead of setting money aside. Your financial plan should always allow for the ramping up of business levels, which might grow gradually, and you should always have contingencies in place.

When calculating how much you'll need to get your business started, be sure to take into account your personal living expenses for at least the first six months of your business start-up. Things can take some time to get rolling and you don't want to put yourself into a financial bind.

3.4.2   Sample Start-Up Budgets

Beginning on the next page are two sample budgets for start-up spa businesses. The values are expressed as a range, from low-end to high-end. This is because there are so many variables that will be particular to a business. For example, if you were able to find a space that had previously been a dentist's office, your renovation costs will be lower since you already have existing "treatment rooms".

On average, this in an industry where you can expect starting your spa to cost you an absolute minimum of $50 per square foot of spa space, $80 or $100 per square foot on average, and more than $100 per square foot when you want to have high-end appeal. This means that a 2,000 square foot spa suggests an extreme low-end start-up cost of $100,000, and a high-end cost of $200,000 and up. And of course, you can always spend more if you like!

Small Spa (1,200 square feet)

	Low-End	High-End
Construction/renovation and decorating	$ 35,000	$ 70,000
Furniture and equipment	20,000	40,000
Initial inventory and supplies	10,000	20,000
Misc. expenses	2,500	17,000
Graphic design/website design	5,000	10,000
Spa consultant	5,000	10,000
Insurance	4,000	6,000
Deposit on lease/down-payment on mortgage	1,500	3,000
Professional fees	2,000	3,000
Marketing/advertising	2,500	10,000
Pre-opening staff training	2,000	3,000
Printing (menus, stationery)	2,000	4,000
Computer software	1,000	2,000
Business licenses and permits	500	500
Voluntary accreditation	500	750
Professional memberships	250	500
Deposit on utilities and phone	250	250
TOTAL	$ 100,000	$ 200,000

Medium/Average Spa (2,000–5000 square feet)

	Low-End	High-End
Construction/renovation and decorating	$ 87,500	$ 157,500
Furniture and equipment	50,000	90,000
Initial inventory and supplies	25,000	45,000
Misc. expenses	24,000	45,000
Graphic design/website design	5,000	10,000
Spa consultant	12,000	20,000
Insurance	6,000	10,000
Deposit on lease/down-payment on mortgage	4,500	7,000
Professional fees	5,000	10,000
Marketing/advertising	8,500	16,000
Pre-opening staff training	8,000	16,000
Printing (menus, stationery)	8,000	12,000
Computer software	2,000	6,000
Business licenses and permits	2,000	2,000
Voluntary accreditation	1,000	1,500
Professional memberships	1,000	2,000
Deposit on utilities and phone	500	500
TOTAL	$ 250,000	$ 450,000

Keep in mind that these are industry averages, and don't take into account your unique vision. For example, if you are planning a "spa express" where clients are in and out for mini-facials in 30 minutes, then maybe you can reduce the size of your treatment rooms and cut your decorating budget. This section will also include some cost-cutting ideas for you to consider.

Ways to Cut Your Costs

There are several ways that you can reduce your expenses in certain areas of your spa development, but you want to make sure that you use them wisely.

To be perfectly honest, starting a spa on a tight budget is not a great idea. If you are having to scrimp and economize just to get your spa up and running, how will you handle anything unexpected in your first year or two of business? How will you handle dips in sales related to circumstances beyond your control, such as weather or economy?

Before you look at cutting costs, first take a look at your overall concept — it's possible that cutting back on square footage or simplifying your menu will allow you to start small comfortably, with room for adjustment, and then grow into the dream spa you can't afford right away.

Most professional spa equipment companies offer leasing agreements, which allows you to pay for your equipment over time and may offer the flexibility of upgrading when new models enter the market. The drawback to leasing is that you have a constant drain of cash in the form of payments, which affects your profitability. And anyone who has ever leased a car can tell you that if you can get a loan from the bank to cover your equipment costs, you'll pay less in the long run.

(In fact, if you are looking for funding to start your spa in general, banks may actually prefer that you purchase equipment, as it contributes to your spa's assets.) If you think leasing is right for you, several suppliers to contact are listed at the end of this guide.

A great way to save money on your budget is to swap services with freelance professionals in the marketing, public relations, web development and business development arenas. For example, offer five free spa visits to a graphic designer, in lieu of payment to design your logo. You are fortunate in having a very attractive service to trade for!

You can also offer the value of positive promotion to other merchants. To get a deal on your lounge area furniture, approach a local artisan or furniture store. Tell them that in exchange for the free use or much reduced purchase of their items, you'll place small placards next to your furnishing with the store name and number on them. It will certainly bring exposure to their business, and save you money on furnishings.

Although you'll be tempted to treat these arrangements casually, any barter exchange should be treated the same as a business agreement. A contract defining what work and exchange is being offered as well as expectations and timelines for both parties should be outlined and signed on the dotted line.

> **TIP:** You may still owe taxes on your bartered services for the amount of money that would have changed hands. Check with your federal tax agency on the matter.

We'll look at how to get free publicity for your spa in Chapter 6, a technique that will save you money on your advertising budget.

3.4.3   Getting Financing

Many new spa owners are those who have money and decide to invest in themselves and this industry by starting their own business, but don't be discouraged if you do not have your own seed money. It is totally possible to get financing with the right plan and the right connections. As to the best way to get financing, according to spa consultant Alexis Ufland, it's this simple: "Write a solid business plan." Possible sources of funding include:

- Banks

- Private investors

- Friends and family

- Your own savings

Bank Loans

Bank loans are the most familiar form of business financing. Getting approval for a bank loan will require a solid credit history that is in good standing and a significant amount of investment capital from your end. Banks understand that any business venture is a risk, so they like to know you're willing to put some of your own money on the table as security.

The bank will want to see your business plan as well as comprehensive financials that are supported by documentation. The bank will also have rigid guidelines for the repayment of the loan, and will probably need sufficient collateral to cover the amounts involved in the event of a default.

> **TIP:** If you are looking for less than $50,000 of funding, banks will generally approach your loan as "personal" and will likely be more interested in your personal credit history than your business plan.

In addition to your business plan, a potential lender will want to see a loan proposal, which outlines specifically how much money is needed, how the money will be used and most importantly, when it will be paid back. It should include:

- How much money you want

- How long it will take you to pay it back

- Details of how you plan to spend it

- How you will get the money to pay it back

- What collateral or assets you have

As many different outlines are available for preparation of a loan proposal, you may want to contact your commercial lender to determine the format needed.

When you prepare this document, ask for a little more money than you need. No matter how good their business plan is, most people underestimate the amount of money they need. It is difficult to go back to the bank and get more money when you've just gotten a loan, and it will make the bank very concerned. Get all you need at once, even if it seems like too much. If you do end up with "extra" then hold onto it, and use that money to begin paying back the loan.

Criteria that will affect whether you get the loan include:

- Your personal experience in the industry

- Your personal credit rating

- Your capacity to pay back loan personally if the business fails

- The value of your collateral

- Your character (as perceived in the community)

- Your personal commitment to the business

- The clarity and completeness of your business plan

- The viability of the business concept

- Your management team

- The suitability of your personality to pressure and responsibilities of business

Criteria that affect you not getting the loan include:

- Your spa concept is considered too risky

- You do not have sufficient collateral

- An insufficient financial commitment on your part

- Incomplete business plan (particularly financial projections)

- You do not appear confident or enthusiastic

Business Lines of Credit

A line of credit is discretionary money lent by a bank for operating expenses. Unlike a loan, a line of credit means you pay interest each month only on what you use and as you pay off the principal it becomes available again, with no need to re-apply. The advantage of a line of credit over a loan is that you usually don't pay the interest on the part of the line of credit that you do not use.

You should establish a line of credit at a bank for your business even if you don't intend to use it. You don't want to have to go through the process of applying for a loan if you only need some short-term cash. You can have, and use, that line of credit for a lifetime. Using a credit card will provide a printed monthly purchasing record for you to easily reconcile and track purchasing as well.

Getting a line of credit (or business credit card) shouldn't be difficult if your personal credit history is good. If you've had bad credit in the past you may run into problems, but it's still possible to get credit. Many credit card companies will issue "deposit backed" cards for those wishing to reestablish or improve spotty credit. Keep in mind that these lines of credit generally have a much higher interest rate than most, so try to pay balances off in full whenever possible.

There's not much more to getting a line of credit than applying at your bank to see if you qualify and if it suits your needs. It should:

- Allow you to select the features that best suit your needs

- Include simplified expense and cash flow management

- Offer optional employee cards with distinct purchasing limits

- Earn Air Miles or some rewards, if possible

Private Investors

If your spa business is a large venture requiring hundreds of thousands of dollars worth of capital, private investors (also known as angel investors) may be an option you'll want to consider.

While these investors may seem "heaven-sent", be aware that many entrepreneurs have been burned by a lack of follow-through on money promised, or long-term requirements that give a portion of the company away as well as decision-making rights.

Private investors, while harder to come by, can be more flexible. They may not want to be muddled in the details and get buried in the paperwork that the bank will request. An investor might also be more willing to share in the involved risks, without having collateral to fall back on.

Are there investors like this out there? It depends on who you ask. "Absolutely," says Neil Ducoff of Strategies Publishing Group. "There is a ton of money and a lot of people with cash who think the stock market does not look good right now."

"Three to five years ago you could have found private investors looking to dump money into the spa business," counters Alexis Ufland. "Now you will be better off going to the bank."

To find angel investors or venture capitalist groups beyond your immediate circle of contacts, you can investigate the resources listed below.

- *Angel Investor News*
  www.angel-investor-news.com

- *Start-Up Junkies Angels Page*
  www.startupjunkies.org/angel.html

- *VFinance*
  www.vfinance.com/home_0.asp

- *Venture Capital in Canada*
  http://strategis.ic.gc.ca/app/sourcesOfFinancing/
  instRegistration/Directory

Personal Savings and Investments

Life Insurance Loans: Depending on how long you've had your life insurance, you can borrow against the accumulated cash value of the policy at little-to-no interest and repaying may or may not be a necessity.

Home Equity Loans:	Interest on a home equity debt is deductible. If your business is high-risk (a new venture vs. an existing business that currently runs with a profit) think long and hard before you put your home at risk. If you couldn't pay back this loan, your house would be in jeopardy.
Borrow Against a Margin Account:	A margin loan allows you to borrow cash from your investments without selling. Under current Federal Reserve rules, you can borrow up to 50 percent of the market value of the stock you own.
401Ks:	Note that penalty fees and taxes equal 20% or more of the accumulated total.
IRAs:	You'll need to pay tax due on the total amount + 10% penalty fee.
Savings Accounts:	Your money, penalty-free.

Family & Friends

Borrowing from friends and family works only if you are absolutely certain that mixing finances with personal relationships will not build bad blood in the future. This is very hard to gauge when you're excited to get your new business going. A formal contract outlining what is being borrowed or invested and what is expected in return and by what timeline is recommended.

You may have a customer who believes in you, or a friend, or a colleague, or a family member. If in your mental rolodex you are flipping through all of your acquaintances and not finding anyone who qualifies as an investor, remember the movie *Six Degrees of Separation*. You might not know anyone who can invest in your business, but chances are you know someone who knows someone who could.

Create the buzz about what you are trying to accomplish and get people on your team. Belief is contagious and the more people who believe in you, the more likely you will find someone willing to back up that belief with some funding.

4. Preparing to Open

Starting any business is a life-changing event, and a spa is no different. Once you have decided to take the plunge, you will be thrust into the excitement, the challenges, and the hectic pace of keeping your opening on schedule. This chapter of the guide is designed to prepare you for the many decisions that will be a part of planning to launch your spa, right up to the first day you open your doors for business.

Let's get started!

4.1 Choose a Location

You may have a location in mind for your spa already, which is great. If not, that's fine too. Just about any space can be converted into a spa, but the truth is that some spaces will convert more easily than others, depending on their prior use.

And you can't just look at how easily you can get renovations done, you need to consider how the location will function to attract and keep clients, both now, five years from now, and twenty-five years from now.

4.1.1   Factors to Consider

Here are several factors you should take into account when searching for your location, be it a plot of land or a corner in a strip mall.

Local Traffic

What is the local foot traffic like? Will people be likely to wander in and request a brochure? Will your spa be visible to passing car traffic? Or alternately, is it in so busy of a location that people won't want to fight traffic to and from their "relaxing" spa experience?

Parking

Is there adequate non-metered parking? You don't want your customers to have to worry about running to the parking meters in mid-relaxation. Some busy urban areas may only have metered parking available, and a maximum of two hours of possible paid time. This is an important and often overlooked consideration!

Surroundings

Are there neighborhoods in the surrounding area? Any noise concerns from neighbors that may interrupt the spa experience? In some cases double-paned windows might be enough to block out noise, but in extreme cases that won't be enough.

One contributing author to this guide mentioned a certain neighborhood in her city where, about one day in every two weeks, the wind changes and there is a horrible smell from a chicken factory that is down the road. You'd never know it unless you were there on that day. For this reason, plan to visit your potential spa location as many times as possible before you commit to it.

A nice neighborhood during the day is not always a nice neighbor-hood by night, either. Your town or city police department should be able to provide you with crime statistics for the region you are consid-ering.

If you're building a spa in a rural location that people must travel to, is the area you've selected a desirable travel destination? Are there enough other things to do in the area that people could make a weekend of it, or that some family members could do other things while others went to the spa?

Space

There are two ways to approach your spa plan — you can decide on a number of treatment rooms, layout of area, etc. and then find a space to match it, or you can find a location you like, and plan your spa with it in mind. The second option, or a little of both, is usually the easiest approach.

For example, if your business plan dictates five wet treatment rooms and five dry treatment rooms and you've found a perfect space that could only house eight total, consider how you could adapt your vi-sion to the space — possibly making two of the rooms multi-purpose would allow you to make this space work.

Your spa consultant, if you are working with one, will be a helpful source of information in deciding if the square footage is sufficient to accommodate what you want to do. Your architect and/or engineer can also clarify details about what can and can't be altered in the space. This section has more information coming up on the technical consid-erations of evaluation a location.

Other Spas in the Area

Are there other spas in a five or ten mile radius? How many? Are they similar or different to what you plan to offer? If your location is a strip mall, does your lease include exclusivity rights to the services you offer? It can sometimes be a good thing to be nearby other spas in a spa "district", but you'll need to be confident that you can edge in and claim a percentage of the market share with your unique approach.

Cost

This is usually the bottom line consideration. It may be tempting to buy or lease something a little bigger than you'd planned, but before you do so, have your accountant punch the adjusted mortgage or lease payments into your financial projections and see how numbers shift. You could be surprised how paying just a little more than you had intended can affect your take-home pay.

> TIP: Don't forget to factor in not just the cost of the purchase, but the cost to maintain. An older building could surprise you with over-the-top heating costs and the like.

4.1.2   Who to Consult with

When you are evaluating a potential location, you will want to make sure that the business you plan is a fit with the location by consulting with the building and construction professionals listed below.

Make sure your facility has the capability to run your equipment during your hours of operation. "If you are going to run stone roasters all day long in seven different rooms," says spa consultant Alexis Ufland, "your architect needs to know."

Your spa consultant will be able to find and hire these contractors for you, or if you are on your own, hire your architect first and let them find the engineers for you. Ideally, you will be working with an architect who has designed spas before, and if you are not working with a spa consultant, a spa-experienced architect is a must.

Architectural Designer   Will advise you on the feasibility of your planned layout, and make suggestions to increase attractiveness and function. Talk to your architect about what you plan to use each room for, and incorporate materials that are suitable to a sometimes humid or wet environment. Ask about sloping floors (and sometimes ceilings) in wet and steam rooms, which aids with moisture control and drainage. Your architect should also check local land-use bylaws for requirements such as occupancy, fire exits, required parking, and number of bathrooms.

Structural Engineer

Can evaluate if the planned location's flooring will be able to support the weight of anything heavy you plan to have or install — usually water-holding things such as hydrotherapy tubs or whirlpools. Since you won't have these items yet, contact the manufacturer for an estimate of their filled weight.

Hydraulic Engineer

Will check to make sure that the plumbing in the building is adequate for your needs — that pipes are large enough, water pressure and supply is high enough, they don't rattle or whine, etc. Your drains will need special consideration, since your clients will be showering off thick, gunky things like mud and clay. Mention any specialty water treatments you have in mind for their consideration.

Electrical Engineer

Will evaluate if the location has enough outlets, if they are located conveniently, and that they can bear the charge of your high-tech equipment. Also ask them to take a look at how the existing lighting matches with your proposed needs.

Mechanical Engineer

Will take a look at the heating and cooling (ventilation) systems, and determine if they will need to be altered, and if so, at what cost. Your system must be flexible enough to keep closed treatment rooms comfortable and not stuffy without freezing the office and reception (or the client stepping out of the shower in the next room!).

"Some of these questions seem like common sense, but still need to be asked," says contributing author Jeremy McCarthy. "When you have been in the industry for a while you will hear the stories of the new spa whose mezzanine did not support the weight of the hydro tub. Or the wet treatment room, which was built beautifully, but the tub did not fit through the door to put it in the room."

4.2 Designing Your Layout

Once you're satisfied that the building meets your needs (or can be modified to do so) you're ready to move on to putting your creative talents to work in your design, construction and decorating phase.

4.2.1 Determining Square Footage

To decide how much space you need for your spa, you need to refer back to your business plan that details the services you want to provide, and how many clients you plan to accommodate at a time to meet your fiscal projections. While the number and type of facilities in your spa is limited only by your budget and imagination, most spas will incorporate some combination of the following into their basic layout:

- Treatment rooms (wet, massage, facial)
- Sauna
- Manicure/pedicure area
- Retail space
- Relaxation area (before and after treatment)
- Locker or change rooms (men's and women's)
- Staff room
- Laundry room
- Reception area
- Washrooms
- Office

In addition to basic space, remember that you need to plan for 1/5 to 1/4 of your square footage to be allotted for internal traffic flow, where clients will come in, pick up their robe, walk to the treatment room, etc. The architectural designer we consulted on this matter suggested that even up to 30 percent is not out of line.

According to an online advice column written by spa design expert Sam Marguelies, the majority of day spas end up between 2,500 and 5,000 square feet. (You can find a link to his excellent advice column on SpaTrade.com in the resources at the end of this guide.)

The size of your treatment rooms is important, and should be based on both function and atmosphere. At a very basic level, you need space for the client, the person performing the treatment, and the equipment and supplies needed. The staff member should be able to move around the room easily while he or she performs the treatment.

> **TIP:** You can contact the manufacturers of the equipment you plan to buy to get dimensions for the larger items, and provide this information to your architect.

You may also want to talk to therapists who will be using the treatment rooms, so they can have input on what has worked or not worked for them in the past.

On a more abstract but just as important level, your treatment rooms should be big enough to keep your clients from feeling claustrophobic once you close the door, and convey an impression of roominess. While the perfect size is linked to your spa and the treatment, as a general rule anything smaller than 10 feet by 10 feet is too small. (Don't overlook the important of the ceiling height in this department, either.)

There is an extreme in making your treatment rooms so big clients don't feel comfortable or private, but more often spa owners try to make them too small to maximize the number of clients that can be processed. Once these decisions are made, you can't go back and change them without a major renovation expense.

If you are trying to save on space, you might be tempted to eliminate the meditation/relaxation room since it doesn't directly generate revenue. Before you do, think about the following:

If you don't offer an enjoyable and relaxing space for clients to move into when their treatments are done, they will be tempted to take their time leaving the treatment room itself. You may be able to book more appointments per day if you can efficiently move clients through your spa without negatively impacting their experience… and in this case, adding perceived value. Not an absolute, but good food for thought.

If you will have a manicure, pedicure, or salon area, your architect will want to know how many stations you plan for. Also make sure that you consult with your architect regarding local law on handicap accessibility, which requires additional square footage in many cases. And finally, don't forget to have room in your locker area for double what your spa can accommodate: both the clients arriving, and those who are leaving!

4.2.2   Layout Tips

When laying out the internal flow of your spa, visualize the space as though you were the customer. Walk through a virtual day in your spa, considering flow of traffic and how you would move from coming in, to relaxing, to getting changed, to your treatment room, etc.

"Ask a lot of questions," suggests Alexis Ufland. "Where do clients pick up their robe and slippers? Where is the manager's office? Which space generates revenue and which does not? Can you use space for multiple functions to generate increased revenues? Can you convert non-revenue-generating space into revenue-generating space by adding retail?"

"Pay attention to the 'Big 3' — my nickname for the big three mistakes that almost *every spa* wishes they would have paid more attention to in design and construction," advises spa director Jeremy McCarthy. "If you do a great job in these three areas, you will be better off than most spas out there." These are:

1.   Sound-proofing

2.   Temperature control

3.   Drainage

You will want to ensure that the following details are adhered to:

- Rooms for any kind of relaxation treatment should be furthest from the registration and changing room areas, where noise is most likely.

- Place the manicure stations or salon services close to reception, where chatter is most likely to occur.

- Changing or locker rooms should offer as much privacy as possible and be gender-exclusive.

- Many spa owners will place the retail area near the registration and payment station, so technicians can place products used on customers at the front for their review prior to checkout. This is not a rule. You know your clients best, and whether this approach is too pushy.

- Ideally the public space of a spa should have a central stereo system playing serene music in addition to each room having its own music equipment.

- Many spa owners consult with a designer who is experienced in Feng Shui, an ancient Chinese practice of space design to live better and feel better!

Of course, there is an idyllic model for layout and then there is reality. The reality is that everything may not be positioned where you'd like it, but when a guest is being pampered in the right way, they will not notice slight noises or subtle inconveniences.

The important thing is that your customers are treated with the utmost care and respect. This is what they will remember most and this is what will keep them coming back to you.

4.2.3 Design and Décor

Spa consultant Sylvia Sepielli told us, "The easiest way to make a million dollars in the spa industry is to start with two million." Funny, but true!

It is easy to spend money building a spa. Spas can include extremely high-end equipment, and it is exceedingly more important to offer something above and beyond the competition. The nicer the experience you wish to create for your guests, the more you need to spend in designing your facility.

Soft wall coverings to soften noise, soundproofed doors and insulation, a central sound system, independent temperature controls for each treatment room, unique lighting and water features to stimulate the senses: all these things cost money. The design of the facility will have a lot to do with the concepts you are based on and what services you wish to offer.

Think in terms of how many rooms you will need and what size, but also think about colors and logo images and how you will brand yourself. The colors you use in your spa can have a huge effect on your clients' mood.

According to an article in *Day Spa Magazine*, day spas are "moving away from marble and stone interiors, toward uniquely individual styles and themes that more closely reflect the people who run the spas and the clients they serve." You can read the whole article, complete with beautiful full-color photos, at **www.dayspamag.com/pdf/ fac_prod_serv/ds0105trends.pdf**.

You may find yourself doing a blend of adapting your facility to your menu concepts, and adapting your menu concepts to your facility. Be creative and do not lose the concepts that make you unique. Or as the facility becomes developed, add to your uniqueness, but do not let it get diluted.

Whatever theme you decide on for your spa's decoration, it should be timeless and come from your heart and your vision. There are many trends that are fashionable right now, but unless you plan to do a massive redesign every few years, your perfectly trendy spa today will be the out-of-date (or worse, out-of-business) spa tomorrow.

Hiring and Working with Contractors

"You will need to learn a little about building and contractors," says consultant Sylvia Sepielli, "and the going rate for construction and materials." To find your architect and contractor, she suggests going to any particular buildings you like, and asking them who did the work.

An architect can recommend a contractor, and there is some benefit to hiring people who have worked well together in the past. But as owner, you have the ultimate say, and you will want to compare prices with the competition. The contractors should be forthcoming with pricing information. They will want to give you information to help you choose them. Talk to at least three before comparing notes. Each one will give you good questions to ask the other two. Get ample references on your contractors.

"It is so important to be onsite with the general contractor during construction," says Alexis Ufland, "and really get involved in day-to-day decisions as the project comes along." And triple-check your equipment specs with your contractors before work begins.

"Managing your money is a real big piece," says Neil Ducoff. "People become so over-extended in the build-out phase that they are broke by the time the doors open."

If you start out behind your budget, it is hard to get back on track. Managing the construction phase and keeping it grounded in reality is the key to being sure there is money left over when the time comes to open the spa.

4.3   Equipment & Supplies

Shopping for equipment and supplies for your spa is like sending a kid into a candy store. There are so many luxury items to choose from and the industry continues to innovate and grow every day. The important thing to remember is to identify what you need first (i.e. what will make you money right away), and then move on to your "wants" when the business income can justify the extra expenses.

4.3.1   Where to Look and How to Choose

Always shop around for the best deals, and bargain with suppliers for competitive rates. Not everything needs to be purchased new, either. With spa businesses popping up out of nowhere and disappearing just as quickly, there is a huge market for barely used equipment.

Many of the suppliers we list at the end of this guide sell used equipment as well, and you can even find deals in your local newspaper or on eBay.

Perhaps the best way to find out about used equipment is by word of mouth. When you meet other owners or spa professionals, ask if they know of any spas that are rumored to be closing soon. If you can get in ahead of time, you may be able to get a deal on the equipment as a lot.

It's important to note that while some pieces of equipment are worth buying used, not all will be. Talk to vendors and/or your spa consultant about what pieces of equipment are most likely to break down or require servicing.

You can find a list of suppliers at the end of this guide, and there are many more out there. If it will mean lowering your bottom line, it helps to negotiate. Remember that value comes in all shapes and sizes, and the lowest price is not always the best deal — look at warranties, training, and service or support with the product as future money-savers too.

Depending on the spa services or amenities you plan to offer, there are many more pieces of equipment to choose from. Many spas offer the complimentary use of a sauna for guests, and tanning equipment is a popular addition to spas these days. If you start with the basics, you can let your therapists/estheticians and your clients guide you to where to expand, be it stone therapy, hydrotherapy tubs, or medical treatments.

There is an excellent article online at Preston Inc. Spa Consulting with free advice about making the right choices in spa equipment, both at start-up and down the road. You can read it at **www.prestoninc.net/ HTML/Pages_New/articles/17_choose_equipment.htm**.

4.3.2 Your Basics

This guide provides an overview of the equipment you will need to run a basic day spa that offers massages, facials, body treatments, manicures and pedicures. Where you go from there is up to you. Your spa consultant will be a big aid in determining what equipment best suits your concept, if you as an owner are just learning what is out there.

Front Desk/Office

- Cash drawer

- Clipboards (for clients to fill out forms)

- Computer

- Fax machine

- Office furniture

- Office supplies

- Payment processing equipment

- Phone

- Printer

- Reception furniture

- Safe

- Salon appointment software or appointment books

- Small bags

- Stationery

Treatment Rooms

- Body cushions or bolsters

- Cabinets/storage

- CD players/sound system and music

- Changing chair

- Electric blankets

- Equipment sterilizers

- Facial equipment

- Facial steamers

- Facial treatment chairs

- Floor mats

- Garbage receptacles

- Heat lamps

- Heated treatment bowls

- Hot towel holders

- Laundry hampers

- Magnifiers

- Massage or treatment table warmers

- Massage tables

- Oil warmer

- Sheets

- Stools

- Supply trolleys

- Table pads

- Timer/small clocks

- Towels

- Treatment products (see below)

- Vichy shower (for wet treatments such as body scrubs)

- Wet treatment tables

Miscellaneous

- Art/decorations
- Candles/aromatherapy
- Coffeemaker
- Disinfectant/cleaning supplies
- Disposable sandals
- Disposable underwear
- Fountains
- Fridge
- Retail and/or private label products
- Robes
- Security system
- Uniforms
- Washing machine and dryer

Salon Supplies

- Cosmetics and brushes
- Hair care products and equipment
- Manicure tables/stations
- Manicure/pedicure equipment
- Pedicure tubs
- Stools/chairs
- Waxing supplies and equipment

4.3.3   Treatment Products

Before you choose a type of skin care or body treatment for your spa, it's important to get to know different types that are out there. If you visit other spas before you open, sample a range of treatments and ask about the products being used.

Take note of scents that are pleasing, or results that are impressive. You can also go online to the suppliers listed at the end of this guide, and contact them to send you samples or have a sales rep visit you.

It's important to find a line of products that is in step with your vision and overall theme for your spa. If you have an eco-theme and can find a line of products that donates cash back from purchases towards saving rain forests, you have likely found a perfect match.

There are skin care lines of products that are designed specifically for spa use, which you can find using the suppliers listed at the end of this guide. The advantage to spa-specific products is that they usually come with step-by step instructions for how to perform the treatment, so you can ensure it is being done right, and consistently, in your spa. You may also be able to save some cash by buying in bulk.

Most product brands will also provide in-store signage and help with product display. Aveda is the most hands-on company we talked with. A commitment to opening an Aveda Concept Spa brings with it experienced design teams who help you with every aspect of opening your spa, from real estate acquisition to global brand marketing. A rep will visit your store and help with layout and product placement. For information visit their "Partner with Us" page at **http://aveda.aveda.com/ grow/partner_with_us.asp**.

Products for Retail

An important additional line of income for your spa business will be in selling retail products. Spa services offer a natural sell-in opportunity that you can't afford to miss out on.

If the budget won't allow much for retail at start-up, try sticking to the basics and offering the skin care products used in your facial treatments and the option for customers to buy the nail color they've selected for the day. As you grow you can consider adding some popular spa brands for retail as well as unique home spa product lines.

Finally, the most beneficial retail strategy you can execute would be private labeling a line of products. "I can attest to the fact that nothing is quite as rewarding as seeing a bottle of product with your company name on it!" says spa owner Kibibi Springs.

This process may take some time selecting, formulating, testing and researching anything that will bear your company's name on it, thus representing your spa environment.

Private label brands should be the primary product used during services in order to build the brand. When a customer buys shampoo with your spa's name on it, she's reminded of your business every time she picks up that bottle! You'll find more about selling retail products in section 5.3.

4.3.4   Working with Suppliers

In addition to all of the employees that work with you in the spa, there are a number of suppliers that make what you do possible. You'll have suppliers that sell spa equipment, supplies and above all else, spa products.

Don't overlook how helpful the vendors themselves can be in helping you evaluate what equipment you'll need to offer the services you select. Your relationship with a vendor is a two-way street: you can both help yourselves to be successful. This is most obvious in the case of a product vendor, since the goal of both the vendor and the spa owner is to sell as much product as possible.

Your product and equipment vendors are in an excellent position to help you find the best way to use their equipment and products in your spa. You have to work together to be sure that you are using them in a way which will identify uniquely with your spa, but the vendors will be able to share what has worked well with other spas.

"I suggest using the vendors as much as possible. Ask them to suggest treatments, help you write your menu, develop training manuals and train your staff. Just remember to stay in the driver's seat and not let them dictate how things are done in your spa. They are there to support you, and in the end should help you to do things the way you feel makes sense for your business," advises spa director Jeremy McCarthy.

There really is no right or wrong answer as to what suppliers to use. The absolute best way to make these choices, aside from referrals, is to attend spa trade shows and ask lots of questions. Speak to sales reps, get samples, and try the products yourself or get your employees' opinions.

4.4   Legal Matters

Your lawyer will be an invaluable part of your start-up and operations. Lawyers offer a range of services to the budding entrepreneur, from advice on insurance, licenses, permits and taxes, to required hiring and firing procedures, to drafting or reviewing contracts.

They may also be able to advise you on raising start-up capital, or negotiate the best lease possible. And of course, a lawyer with previous experience helping would-be spa owners will make sure you are getting someone who really knows the ins and outs of opening a spa.

According to the website Nolo.com, most lawyers typically charge anywhere from $150 to $250 an hour to answer routine legal questions. This means that the more you know about legal matters yourself, the less you'll pay in the long run.

While this section offers an introduction to legal matters, you don't want to be doing this without an attorney. You can help yourself with some self-study in the area. Nolo.com publishes a *Legal Guide for Starting and Running a Small Business*, written by Fred S. Steingold. The website at **www.nolo.com** is also a valuable resource for free advice about starting and running a business.

4.4.1   Licensing and Permits

As with any business, the one thing you never want to overlook or be without are the correct licenses and permits required to maintain your good standing. Here's a checklist of the red tape required to keep your business operational. Specifications vary from city, to state, to country so be sure to speak to your lawyer or spa consultant about the requirements specific to your spa's location.

Federal Licenses

- EIN (Employer Identification Number) from the IRS

State/County Licenses

- Sales and Use or State Tax Permit to collect and remit sales tax

- State Business Registration (LLC and corporations must register with the Secretary of State Office or Department of Corporations)

- Fictitious Business Name must be registered with county or state

- Department of Labor registration to ensure you follow laws for unemployment, workers' compensation

- Your State Occupational Safety division may require proof of an injury and illness prevention plan

- Health Department license - health inspector will come out during your build-out phase and approximately once per year thereafter to ensure that your establishment is up to health code

Town/City Licenses & Permits

- Business License

- Building Permits

- Fire Inspection

- Police Permit (some cities require that spa businesses maintain a police commission permit license so that they can keep tabs on brothel-type activity)

Employee Licenses

You must have the correct licenses and certifications on file for each employee or subcontractor who works in your spa according to their specific expertise. You also need to acquire proof that they are legally eligible to work in the U.S.

Canadian-Specific Licenses

Canadians will need to look into the following in their region:

- Goods and Services Tax (GST)

- Municipal business license

- Provincial licenses (business and employment)

You can also go to the Canada Revenue Agency website to learn more about business taxes. Visit **www.cra-arc.gc.ca/tax/business/menu-e.html**.

4.4.2   Naming Your Business

You'll want to choose a name that reflects you and your spa concept in some way. In most cases, your business name should:

- Indicate what you do (e.g. Spa Pleasures)

- Be easy to remember and pronounce

- Attract customers

- Be unique

- Not be currently in use by someone else

You might think naming the spa in honor of your grandmother is a wonderful tribute, but how will spa-goers perceive "Prudence's Spa"? Think it over and choose your name carefully, with your target market set firmly in your sights.

In most jurisdictions, if you operate under anything other than your own name, you are required to file for a fictitious name. It's usually just a short form to fill out and a small filing fee that you pay to your state or provincial government. You can find links to the appropriate departments at **www.sba.gov/hotlist/businessnames.html**.

Before registering a fictitious name, you will need to make sure it does not belong to anyone else. You certainly wouldn't want to spend your initial investment money, only to find out you couldn't legally operate under a name you had chosen because someone else owns the trademark.

Alexis Ufland recommends thinking now about whether you might some day want to expand into multiple locations. If there is even a remote possibility, now is the time to come up with the clever name that will follow your spa to each fabulous new location, and make sure it is not already in use in any of the areas you may want to expand into.

You can do an online search of the federal trademark database at **www.uspto.gov** to determine whether or not a name has already been registered. In Canada, two sites that specialize in business name searches are NUANS at **www.nuans.com** and CorpCanada Services Inc. at **www.corpcanada.ca**.

4.4.3   Insurance

From the time you sign a lease or purchase a building, you will need some sort of insurance in place. There are different types of coverage you will need depending on your situation, and spa insurance has a reputation for not being cheap. You need to talk to an insurance professional to find out which types of insurance you will need for your spa, but below you'll find the most common ones.

- *Business Premises and Contents Insurance:* This will cover your actual spa and contents. If you rent space, the landlord/owner would normally pay for insurance on the property.

- *Product or Service Liability Insurance:* Protects you in the event you are sued by a client for nonperformance of a service or a product and any liability arising from the nonperformance. Note that if you are "renting" space to your service providers, you may want to ask them to carry their own coverage as well.

- *General Liability:* Covers injury to clients and employees on your premises or elsewhere either in the performance of duties for the company or involving activities of the company.

- *Life, Disability, Accident and Illness Insurance:* Provides you with a source of income is you should become seriously ill or disabled and unable to run your business, or provides for your family if you are their main source of income.

- *Business Use Vehicle Insurance:* Must be obtained for cars and other vehicles used in the conduct of your business, such as in a mobile spa.

- *Business Interruption* or *Loss-of-Income Insurance:* This will allow you to continue to pay the bills if you business should have to be closed down by damage due to fire, flood, or other catastrophe.

- *Partnership Insurance:* Protects you against suits arising from actions taken by other partners in your business.

Here's are some resources you can use to learn more about business insurance in the U.S. and Canada:

- *Determining Your Insurance Needs*
  (Click on "Management and Planning Series" and then scroll down to #17.)
  http://www.sba.gov/tools/resourcelibrary/publications

- *Small Business Insurance: What You Need and Why You Need It*
  (Click on "Legal," then scroll down to the "How to Protect Your Business in 4 Easy Steps". Scroll down to "3.-Insure Your Business" and look for the article link.)
  www.canadabusiness.ca/alberta/main.cfm

In the spa industry, the use of a client liability waiver is relatively common. You and your lawyer can draft a form similar to the sample on the next few pages, in which each client will state their current medical conditions, and release you from any liability arising from the spa treatment aggravating these conditions.

Whether or not this form would protect you in court is debatable, but it helps your service providers make an informed decision about whether or not certain treatments are appropriate, given the client's condition.

Sample Client Questionnaire

Name: _____

           Last   *First*   *Middle*

Date of Birth: _____ Sex: M / F

Address: _____

Emergency Contact: _____ Phone: _____

Please circle "YES" or "NO" and provide additional details where required or requested.

1. Do you have any allergies?   NO   YES
    Please list:

    _____

    _____

2. Are you currently taking any prescribed   NO   YES
    medication?

    List and give reason:

    _____

    _____

3. Have you ever had an epileptic seizure?   NO   YES

4. Do you have or have you ever had high
    blood pressure?   NO   YES

    List any medication:

    _____

    _____

5. Do you have, or have you ever had,   NO   YES
    a heart condition?

    Please provide details, date, if surgery was performed, etc.:

    _____

    _____

6. Do you have asthma?   NO   YES

    If so, do you use an inhaler?   NO   YES

    List type of medication in inhaler: _____

7. Have you had a concussion or other   NO   YES
    head injury in the past three years?

    If so, describe and give date(s):

    _____

    _____

8. Are you currently experiencing neck and   NO   YES
    back problems, or any other joint and
    muscle pain?

    Please provide details:

    _____

    _____

9. Have you recently had any skin conditions,   NO   YES
    cuts or infections?

    Please provide details:

    _____

    _____

10. Are you currently pregnant?   NO   YES

    If yes, due date: _____

The questions on this form have been answered completely and truthfully to the best of my knowledge. In signing this form, you are waiving the spa from any liability concerning the reoccurrence or further damage to an existing injury or ailment.

Signature: _____

Date: _____

4.4.4   Employee Contracts

You will want to have your lawyer prepare contracts for each of your spa employees to sign, in order to protect your client list and your business trade secrets. Otherwise you leave yourself open to your employees of today becoming your competitors of tomorrow, armed with your best secrets and their loyal clients. It would be nice to think this never happens, but it does!

Your lawyer can help you draft a spa-specific contract that stipulates that your employees will adhere to a non-compete clause, which states that they will not open a competitive business within a given radius from your location (5 miles, 10 miles, or whatever seems reasonable in your geographic region) within a certain amount of time, such as a year or more.

In some cases, spa owners will stipulate that their past employees cannot even work at a competing business within that vicinity, but this is dicey territory for a start-up spa. It may seem to protect your interests, but it may also prevent you from finding employees willing to sign such an agreement when they don't know you or your spa that well.

They can also be cost-prohibitive to enforce — as in, is it really worth thousands of dollars in legal fees to pursue one of your employees because they started working for the spa down the street?

You can also ask your lawyer about clauses regarding employees contacting your clientele should they decide to leave your employ of their own will, and protection of your trade secrets and unique approaches. No contract is airtight, but this should help protect you and your hard-earned business.

A sample contract can be found on the next page that you can use for inspiration, or bring to your lawyer to amend or adapt for your purposes. This contract is provided as a sample only; a lawyer should always review any contract before you use it for your business.

Sample Employee Contract

This agreement of employment is being made between
_____ and Splendid Spas. Employment for the
position(s) of _____ will commence on
_____.

All employees of Splendid Spas are to adhere to the following
terms:

1. **Company Policies:** The employee shall comply with all
   stated performance standards, policies, rules, and regulations. The employee shall also comply with future amend-
   ments to the said performance standards, policies, rules and
   regulations.

2. **Working Hours:** The employee agrees to arrive on time for
   work and be able for work for 9 hours each working day
   between the hours of _____ and _____. The 9 hours
   includes a one-hour, non-paid lunch break.

3. **Salary:** Upon commencement of employment, the employee
   shall be paid the agreed upon salary of $ _____ on a
   bi-weekly basis.

4. **Vacation:** The employee shall be entitled to two weeks paid
   vacation each year, commencing after one year of employment.

5. **Proprietary Information:** Employees of Splendid Spas agree
   to hold proprietary secrets and business information in confidence. Any breach of this could result in termination.

6. **Non-compete Clause:** As an employee of Splendid Spas, you
   agree that at any time during the during the period of your
   employment, and for a 24-month period following ceasing
   to be an employee, that you will not compete directly or in-
   directly with this business within a ____ mile radius of this
   business. This includes freelance or contract work.

7. **Termination of the Agreement:** At any time Splendid Spas may terminate this employee contract under terms such as: failure to adequately perform duties, financial hardship of the company, or any other reason within the terms of employment standards.

By signing this employee contract, the employee agrees to all of the above terms in good faith.

Signed this _____ day of _____ 20_____.

_____   _____
Splendid Spas   *Employee*

4.5 Your Menu of Services

Your menu of services is what will define your spa to clients. In many cases, a client's first trip to the spa will be as a result of receiving a gift certificate that was accompanied by your menu. People will also share the menu with friends, leave them on coffee tables, and receive them as part of advertising packages. The bottom line is, your menu is the voice your spa has to speak to new clients. Take the time to make it a powerful tool.

4.5.1 A Unique Look and Feel

Your menu of services should be a powerful pamphlet that inspires relaxation just by holding it in your hands. It should also convey the unique ambiance and feel that you have patterned in your décor, your mission statement, and even the uniforms your service providers will wear.

While every menu will be unique, we will explain in this section the features that the majority of spa menus will have in common.

Get Inspired

Inspiration for your menu of services can come from any number of places.

Chances are you have amassed a collection of them as you pondered opening your own spa, but if you haven't, go out right away and collect a few from the local spas. Lay the menus out in front of you, and note the similarities and differences in each. Think about the following:

- What size and shape are they?

- What colors are used?

- How many pages are they?

- What stock of paper are they printed on — is it glossy, or does it have a linen-look? Raised type?

- How is the brochure bound? Staples? Spiral?

- What type of font was used? Is it fairly legible?

- Are there pictures? If so, of what?

Finally, note the unique features that set each menu apart. One of our authors mentioned an eye-catching spa menu she picked up, in which all of the types of services were printed on small sheets of thin, almost papyrus-like paper that nested inside an envelope shaped like a money-holder greeting card. The font was small and scripted, and the color was a pale beige.

In contrast, on the same day she picked up a menu that was completely on the other end of the spectrum: a square, black-and-white spiral-bound menu printed on heavy cardstock, with bold font and inspirational sayings throughout.

While these two menus had many features in common, they gave off very different (and strong) impressions of what their spa and spa experience would be like. It's most important that you make sure your menu of services, whatever it ends up like, is anything but bland.

What to Include

Your menu will convey information about each of the services your spa offers: a description of the service, usually a price, and, most importantly, the benefits of receiving that service. Think in terms of relaxation, healing, beautification, smoothness, or whatever you think clients are after. We listed a number of benefits of each typical spa service for you in section 2.2.

Before writing your menu text, consider the term "menu" for a bit — it evokes the idea of dining out. The language you use in your spa menu will be similar to what you are used to reading in a restaurant. The peas are never just peas; they are "mouth-watering, juicy bursts of sweetness." This is the kind of language used in most spa menus as well, as you'll see in the sample menu in this section.

When you choose services for your spa, make sure that each service is unique, and different enough from others you plan to offer. If you find that two services seem to be too close in nature, choose the one that best suits your spa, is most economical to offer, or is the best fit with the products you'll use or sell. Also think about which services will come together best as packages, and select accordingly.

TIP: Plan to reprint your menu from time to time. Reprinting the menu is an opportunity to remove treatments which have not sold and maybe add something more marketable.

Many spa brochures will include a brief section on spa etiquette that includes requests such as asking guests to arrive on time or a bit early, and to respect the spa environment by turning off their cell phones. This is also an appropriate place to state your cancellation policy, hours of operation, and reservation procedure.

Where appropriate, you may want to include pictures, artwork or inspirational sayings that convey the mood or ambiance of your spa. The colors you choose should also evoke an image of your spa (although black and white can be effective too). You may also want to use the logos of any brand-name products you spa is affiliated with, to inspire consumer confidence.

When you have your service definitions and an overall look planned for the menu, take the project to a graphic design specialist to prepare for print. Expect to pay a minimum of $50 an hour for this service, and a few thousand dollars on having your menu printed. If you don't have a graphic designer, a full-service printer can lay out your files for you.

Packaging Services to Sell

Packaging your spa services together for a reduced price is a great way to sell your clients additional services they might not otherwise purchase. Typical packages include bride-to-be and mother-to-be, as well as anti-aging or total relaxation. Linking your packages with events or circumstances in life, from weddings and motherhood to stress and aging, forges connections that make the purchase of a particular package seem "obvious" given the circumstances.

Take the time to come up with names for your packages and services that convey a mood or feel. "Standard Pedicure" is less likely to sell to clients than "Foot Fantasy" or something in that vein. Match your treatment names to your targeted clients, too, be they male, female, young, aging, etc. They should evoke an emotion from the client.

To encourage retail sales and add value to your packages, consider offering a $10 credit towards any retail purchase of spa products with any package purchase. This gets people who would not otherwise make a purchase to do so, rather than "wasting" their $10 credit.

4.5.2   A Sample Menu

Contributing author Jeremy McCarthy, who is the current spa director of the Spa at La Costa in Carlsbad, California, was kind enough to grant FabJob the permission to reprint the La Costa Spa menu of services here in this guide. It is included on the next few pages.

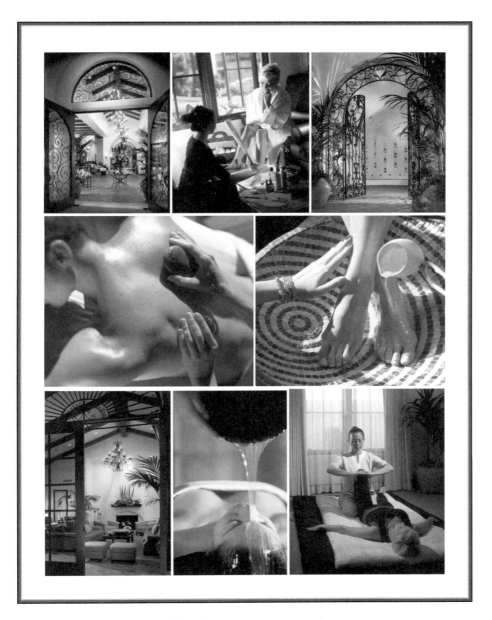

Sample spa menu, page 1

Immerse yourself in AGUA de la VIDA

With soothing whirlpools, thundering Roman Waterfalls, a purifying steam room and more, AGUA de la VIDA -"the Water of Life", is an experience unique to La Costa. A series of water elements combined with a professional exfoliating body scrub, it is the perfect prelude to a spa treatment, or an exhilarating journey all its own. Complimentary with most spa services or available á la carte, AGUA de la VIDA also includes access to the Spa's lounge, cedar sauna, private sunbathing area and outdoor courtyard amenities.

VIP SPA JOURNEYS FOR TWO

Indulge in the royal treatments available within our lavish VIP Spa Suites, luxuriously outfitted with side-by-side massage tables, fireplace, private shower and bathroom, telephone, television and many other amenities – all accompanied by an outdoor patio with private whirlpool.

ROMANTIC JOURNEY FOR TWO · 2 Hours

Unlimited day use of the spa · AGUA de la VIDA · 50-minute La Costa Massage for two · Bottle of champagne · Fresh Carlsbad strawberries with chocolate truffles · One hour of additional leisure time in your VIP Spa Suite

HARMONY JOURNEY FOR TWO · 2 1/2 Hours

Unlimited day use of the spa · AGUA de la VIDA · 80-minute La Costa Massage for two · Spa Café lunch for two · Bottle of champagne · Fresh Carlsbad strawberries with chocolate truffles · One hour of leisure time in the VIP Spa Suite

DELUXE SPA SUITE JOURNEY · 3 Hours

Unlimited day use of the spa · AGUA de la VIDA · Two 50-minute California Renewal body treatments · 50-minute La Costa Massage for two · Spa Café lunch for two · Two plush keepsake spa robes · Bottle of champagne · Fresh Carlsbad strawberries with chocolate truffles · One hour of additional leisure time in your VIP Spa Suite

Sample spa menu, page 2

DAY SPA JOURNEYS

Includes unlimited day use of the Spa at La Costa.

SIGNATURE SENSORY JOURNEY · Half day
AGUA de la VIDA · Begin with an "Awakening of Tastes", followed by a unique sensory journey: 50-min. Thai Massage, Chakra Balancing, Crystal Therapy, Dry Body Buffing and 50-min. Aromatherapy Massage, Chakra Chime Sound Therapy, Meditations and Deep Breathing. Spa Café lunch included.

SPA LEGENDS · Full day
AGUA de la VIDA · 50-minute California Renewal body treatment · 50-minute La Costa Massage · 50-minute Skin Awakening Facial · Spa Café lunch · Manicure and Pedicure · Shampoo and Style at the Yamaguchi Salon

CALIFORNIA ESCAPE · Half day
AGUA de la VIDA · 50-minute California Renewal body treatment · 50-minute La Costa Massage · 50-minute Skin Awakening Facial · Spa Café lunch

TRANQUILITY · Half day
AGUA de la VIDA · 50-minute La Costa Massage · 50-minute Skin Awakening Facial

ANTI-AGING · Half day
AGUA de la VIDA · 50-minute Seaweed Body Wrap · 80-minute Coastal Stone Massage · 80-minute Classic Epicuren Facial · Spa Café lunch

MEN'S DAY · Half day
AGUA de la VIDA · 50-minute Golf Champions Massage · 50-minute Men's Executive Facial · Spa Café lunch

INDULGENCE · Half day
AGUA de la VIDA · 50-minute California Renewal body treatment · 80-minute La Costa Massage · 50-minute Skin Awakening Facial · Spa Café lunch

INVIGORATION · Half day
AGUA de la VIDA · 50-minute California Vegetable Clay Wrap · 80-minute Thai Massage · 50-minute Custom La Costa Facial · Spa Café lunch

INSPIRATION · Half day
AGUA de la VIDA · 80-minute Spanish Herbal Body Rub · 50-minute La Costa Massage · 50-minute Skin Awakening Facial · Spa Café lunch

MASSAGES

LA COSTA MASSAGE · 50 minutes · 80 minutes
Your massage therapist will use a specific aromatherapy blend and a variety of massage techniques to customize your spa journey.

COASTAL STONE MASSAGE · 80 minutes
Using smooth hot and cool stones hand-selected from the Pacific Coast, your massage therapist uses the penetrating heat of the stones to melt away stress, while relieving tense muscles and sore joints, bringing balance and healing to your body.

GOLF CHAMPIONS MASSAGE · 50 minutes · 80 minutes
Your massage therapist uses therapeutic techniques targeting the areas of your body impacted most by your golf game or other sports activities.

THAI MASSAGE · 80 minutes / $205
This ancient technique of Buddhist origin incorporates stretching and zen-line compression to open energy channels and increase range of motion. It is helpful in improving performance in golf or other sports.

SHIATSU MASSAGE · 50 minutes
Shi meaning 'thumb' and Atsu 'pressure', this ancient form of Eastern acupressure massage revitalizes the body by releasing muscle tension and reducing fatigue.

FOUR HANDS MASSAGE · 50 minutes
This indulgent journey pampers you with two massage therapists and four hands that simultaneously choreograph the ultimate massage.

REFLEXOLOGY MASSAGE · 50 minutes · 80 minutes
Your massage therapist brings comfort and relaxation to your entire body, while applying pressure upon the reflex points of your hands and feet.

HYDROTHERAPY MASSAGE · 50 minutes
While blissfully soaking and steaming in our state-of-the-art Hydrotherapy Tub, enjoy an essential oil scalp treatment and a unique 30-minute hydrotherapy massage.

BATH AND MASSAGE DUET · 50 min. · 80 min.
Your choice of our Oligomer Bath, Aromatherapy Bath, or Spanish Herbal Bath, followed by a therapeutic 30-min. or 50-min. body massage.

SUITE HEART'S MASSAGE · 50 min. · 80 min.
Share your spa journey with that special someone with a side-by-side massage inside our luxurious and private couple's massage suite.

MOTHER'S MASSAGE · 50 minutes · 80 minutes
This soothing and gentle massage eases muscle tension and fatigue during pregnancy, focusing on the special needs of the mother-to-be.

Sample spa menu, page 3

RELAXING BATHS & WATER THERAPIES

These soothing baths include a conditioning hair and scalp treatment. For the ultimate experience, combine with a 50-minute massage.

OLIGOMER MINERAL BATH
Let your stresses melt away in this restorative mineral bath and feel the result of softened skin.

AROMATHERAPY BATH
Delicate bath salts infused with essential oils soften your skin and help calm your body and spirit.

SPANISH HERBAL BATH
Fragrant sage, lavender, and rosemary oils moisturize your skin and invigorate your senses.

BODY CARE

SPANISH HERBAL BODY RUB · 80 minutes
Native Spanish herbs (fragrant sage, lavender, and rosemary) unite with pure olive oils during this indulgent massage and skin polishing. Your body is then luxuriously enveloped in a fragrant herbal wrap while your scalp is massaged and deeply conditioned with sage oil.

LA COSTA DESIGNER TREATMENT · 80 minutes
A warm herbal wrap envelopes your body while your scalp, neck and face are massaged. Self-heating effervescent mud is then applied to melt away tension in your back and feet while your therapist extensively massages your forearms, hands, feet, legs and back.

CALIFORNIA RENEWAL · 50 minutes
Smoother, younger skin is revealed after receiving this invigorating full-body exfoliation, which is followed by a soothing and healing aloe and arnica flower body wrap. A moisturizing veil of lotion, using your choice of indulging, invigorating or inspiring scents, gives your skin a healthy glow. Please refrain from shaving or sunbathing 24 hours prior to treatment.

VEGETABLE CLAY WRAP · 50 minutes
An exfoliating massage cream prepares your skin to receive California's therapeutic, mineral-rich clays, which help to restore moisture and draw out impurities. Luxuriate in a rinse under six shower heads of our Vichy Rainshower.

SEAWEED BODY WRAP · 50 minutes
This all-natural sea algae wrap infuses essential sea minerals and antioxidant vitamins renowned for deeply nourishing the skin. Luxuriate in a rinse under six shower heads of our Vichy Rainshower.

CITRUS BODY SCRUB · 30 minutes
A combination of unique sea salts and specialty spa oils are gently massaged over the body to exfoliate dry surface skin. The Citrus Body Scrub is followed by a luxurious rinse under the six shower heads of our Vichy Rainshower. Please refrain from shaving or sunbathing 24 hours prior to treatment.

REVITALIZING LEG TREATMENT · 30 minutes
Revitalize tired legs with a gentle exfoliation and energizing leg mask, followed by an application of a soothing spa gel that will help reduce any swelling and congestion.

BEAUTIFUL BRONZING · 30 minutes
Enjoy a flawless, natural-looking tan after two passes of premium spray-on sunless tanning product. Please refrain from shaving or sunbathing 24 hours prior, or showering up to 6 hours after.

DELUXE BRONZING · 50 minutes
Indulge while your therapist applies exfoliating massage cream, followed by multiple passes of premium spray-on sunless tanning product to achieve that radiant tropical tan.

Sample spa menu, page 4

FACIALS

50-minute facials include a hand and shoulder massage. • 80-minute facials include a scalp, shoulder, and hand massage.

LA COSTA CUSTOM FACIAL • 50 minutes • 80 minutes
During this pampering facial, your esthetician will choose from three intensive masks best suited for your skin type:

- Luminous "C" and "Sea" Mask - hydrates dry skin using Vitamin C and seaweed.
- Plantomer Mask with Propolis - nourishes with natural Propolis, algae and minerals.
- Oxy-Vital Mask - helps renew skincells using aloe, elastin, collagen and azulene.

SKIN AWAKENING FACIAL • 50 minutes
Achieve healthy, radiant skin with a deep cleansing, relaxing facial steam, and gentle extractions, followed by a stress-relieving shoulder, neck and face massage, and purifying facial mask.

AYURVEDIC FACIAL • 60 minutes • 80 minutes
An ancient East Indian facial using dosha-specific oils. Included is an Ayurvedic facial massage focusing on the marma points. The 80-minute facial includes meditative breathing techniques to stimulate your body's own self-healing powers.

CLASSIC EPICUREN FACIAL • 80 minutes
An enzyme-activated, scientifically-proven skincare system that helps diminish the appearance of wrinkles. Your complexion will glow with the cleaner, healthier radiance of more youthful skin.

MEN'S EXECUTIVE FACIAL • 50 minutes
Perfect for men's skin care needs. The face will be thoroughly cleansed and steamed, followed by a relaxing shoulder, neck, face and hand massage.

SIGNATURE AYURVEDIC THERAPIES
At the CHOPRA CENTER for WELL BEING

For more information, please visit www.chopra.com or call 888.424.6772.

ODYSSEY ENLIVENING THERAPY
• 35 minutes - 2 Chopra therapists
• 70 minutes - 1 Chopra therapist
• 75 minutes - 2 Chopra therapists

Experience a blissful journey through your senses with a sampling of five Ayurvedic signature therapies: Garshana - to exfoliate; Abhyanga - to nourish; Vishesh - to relax; Marma and Aromatherapy - to enliven.

ABHYANGA • abee-yan-ga
• 35 minutes - 2 Chopra therapists
The Abhyanga is a choreographed rhythmic friction massage performed by two therapists to loosen ama (toxins), increase circulation and enhance the immune system.

VISHESH • vi-shesh
• 35 minutes - 2 Chopra therapists
The Vishesh is a firm massage with long, deep rhythmic strokes performed by two therapists to relieve tension and detoxify the channels of circulation.

GANDHARVA • gaan-dar-va • 70 minutes
Surrounded by the healing sounds of a crystal singing bowl, our signature Gandharva therapy joins an Ayurvedic body massage with energy and Marma therapy to restore balance.

PIZICHILLI • pitzi-chilli
• 75 minutes - 2 Chopra therapists
Our premier and most luxurious therapy, the gentle and rhythmic Pizichilli offers a continuous stream of warm, herbalized oils massaged into your body by two therapists. Profoundly relaxing and deeply purifying.

SAHASWARA • sah-hah-swah-ra
• (Thousand-Petal Lotus) • 90 minutes
The Sahaswara therapy incorporates a full-body rhythmic oil massage with light stretching movements and a guided visualization recorded by Deepak Chopra. This massage helps open the vital energy centers in the body using aromatherapy and crystals. Discover your unfolding of the thousand-petal lotus flower.

Sample spa menu, page 5

FENG SHUI BEAUTY
At the YAMAGUCHI SALON at LA COSTA
Complimentary Feng Shui Beauty Consultations are available daily.

THE ART OF HAIR Includes a complimentary Feng Shui beauty consultation.
Designer Cut · Sr. Designer Cut · Children's Cut under 12 yrs · Feng Shui Cut with Billy Yamaguchi

MANICURE & PEDICURE RITUALS

HAYAI TSUME · manicure / pedicure
Cleansing of the hands or feet, nail shaping, cuticle conditioning, application of emollient balm and polish.

INDULGING MANICURE
Hayai Tsume manicure with an indulgent hand and lower arm massage, exfoliation and paraffin dip.

YAMAGUCHI TEA MANICURE
Hayai Tsume with soy milk soak, green tea clay masque, and pampering massage with green tea lotion.

YAMAGUCHI TEA PEDICURE
Same procedure as Tea Manicure, except the pampering is focused on your feet.

SHOGUN PEDICURE
After a warm salt soak, the gentle pouring of cool water invigorates tired soles, and a bamboo massage aids circulation. Yin-Yang Gel is massaged onto feet and lower legs. Nails are conditioned, trimmed, buffed or polished, and moisturized with Yamaguchi crème.

YIN YANG PEDICURE
This aromatherapy pedicure uses fragrant essential oils, followed by exfoliation, paraffin dip, an incredible leg and foot massage, nail conditioning, emollient balm and polish application.

PARAFFIN TREATMENT
Enjoy a luxurious hand or foot scrub, hot towel treatment and pampering hand and arm, or foot and leg massage with essential oils and crèmes.

COLOUR, STYLE & MAKEUP
One Process Colour • Partial Highlights • Full Highlights • Correction Colour • Style & Dry • Style & Dry with Flat Iron • Formal Styling / Up Do • Bridal Formal Styling or Up Do • Bridal Makeup • Makeup Application • Makeup Lesson •

WAXING
Eyebrow, Lip, or Chin Wax • Facial Wax

HAIR TREATMENTS
Bamboo Conditioning Treatment / With Essential Oil Scalp Treatment

---

GENERAL SPA INFORMATION

SPA AT LA COSTA
800.729.4772 • 760.931.7570 • lacosta.com

YAMAGUCHI SALON
800.729.4772 • 760.438.0551 • yamaguchifengshui.com

THE CHOPRA CENTER
888.424.6772 • 760.494.1600 • chopra.com

GIFT CARDS · To order a customized spa gift card, please call 760.931.7570 or visit lacosta.com

GROUP EVENTS · To reserve a private spa event or special occasion, please call 760.804.7452.

SPA ETIQUETTE

ENSURE A SERENE ENVIRONMENT · Please turn cell phones and pagers off before arrival to preserve the tranquility of your spa experience. Smoking is not permitted.

GRATUITIES · Gratuities are not included in spa treatment prices; monetarily rewarding your therapists is at your discretion and always very much appreciated.

Prices, hours and services are subject to change.

Sample spa menu, page 6

Sample spa menu, page 7

4.5.3   How to Set Your Prices

Setting your service prices is a balancing act that juggles what your clients are willing to pay, what your own costs are, and how much a particular service is in demand. These are not constants, so expect your prices to fluctuate as the factors that affect them shift. And of course, the bottom line is not just breaking even, but being profitable.

According to 2004 ISPA data, the average price of a spa treatment in the U.S. is $75. We have also included average retail prices for the common spa services listed in section 2.2 of this guide. What your spa fees will be — the amount you charge for each service — is extremely important to the success or failure of your spa.

Here are some factors to consider when setting your prices:

Covering Your Costs

How you determine the price of a particular service should be based on the following costs to you as owner.

- How much it costs you in labor: In general, esthetician services will cost you less to offer than massage therapist services, since you can pay them less per hour. Unique services requiring specialized training will cost you more.

- How much it costs you in product: If you are offering body treatments with exotic ingredients imported from far-away lands, your clients should expect to pay more.

- How much it costs you in overhead: You can't forget to take into account the indirect expenses of running your spa, which each service must cover a portion of. A service that drains electricity or uses water will cost you more to offer.

A lot of small business owners feel guilty about charging too much more than what they are paying to provide the service, but you should try to achieve the healthiest margin the market will support. After all, if your cost to provide a service fluctuates (say electricity costs go through the roof next winter) your clients won't want to suddenly pay more. If you have built a buffer into the price, you can better absorb the inevitable ups and downs of providing a service.

Perceived Value and Your Clients

In many businesses, your prices need to be very competitive for you to be successful. For example, customers know that they can buy milk at one store, and it's the same milk they can get at the store on the next block. Once they know the milk is the same, the determining factors come down to convenience, and cost.

Spa services, by their nature, are generally perceived as a "luxury", and are therefore a bit different from selling milk or bread. You have a bit more wiggle room when it comes to setting your prices if you can set your services apart somehow. Your services can be unique in themselves, or in the way they are presented.

Perhaps you have a local musician playing classical guitar in the relaxation room. Perhaps all your service providers also know ancient chants they can use while performing a service. Or maybe it's as simple as a perfect cup of tea while the client relaxes, or the fluffiest robes in town.

By keeping up-to-date with trends in the spa industry, and investing in training for your best employees, your spa can offer services just as they are coming into vogue. If you can keep pace with what's going on in trend-setting centers like New York, LA and Toronto, you will bring that glamour and luxury home to your clients, and they'll love you for it.

> **TIP:** There is a difference between trends and fads. Trends are general directions of consumer preference, while fads are here today and gone tomorrow. Before you invest in expensive equipment to offer a new and exciting service, think about whether you are buying into a trend or a fad.

Rate Your Degree of Luxury

A factor in determining the cost of your spa services is related to what experts in the field call your "degree of luxury". That is, where does your spa fit into your market? Are your clients extremely wealthy? Middle-class? What is their average income? What level of service will they expect?

A good way to gauge your degree of luxury is to look at your planned start-up costs as explained in section 3.4, which ranged from low-end to high-end. If you built a high-end spa, you will need to offer high-end services, with a high-end price tag. If you are marketing a more affordable spa service, then your prices will reflect that.

4.6   Hiring Your Team

It is difficult to budget and forecast how much your spa will spend on labor dollars without having an understanding of how many hours of labor you will need in each area. Here is some information that will help you in planning for your team of spa employees.

4.6.1   Who to Hire

The number and type of staff you initially hire for your spa will be determined as part of your business planning, and will reflect your projected number of customers per service per day. The staff you hire should be in step with your chosen specialty or niche. Remember, not all spas have to offer massage therapy, and not all have medical treatments on the menu.

As owner you may or may not be involved hands-on in the hiring, but you should definitely be the one to set hiring policies and make sure they are followed. Spa businesses usually have a higher-than-average turnover, so hiring will continue to be an ongoing part of your spa operations. Section 5.2 has information about managing and motivating a happy staff to keep your hiring needs to a minimum.

Possible Positions

Positions you may want to hire one or more people for include:

- Receptionist and/or retail salesperson

- Massage therapist(s)

- Esthetician(s)

- Makeup artist

- Hair stylist/barber

- Hair coloring specialist

- Nail technician

- Spa technician

- Housekeeper

- Assistant director

- Spa director

- Fitness consultant

- Diet consultant

- Nurse or doctor

You can practice filling out a staffing schedule (use a simple grid with spa positions on one side, and hours of operation across the other side) in a number of different ways to see what meshes best with your hours of operation — if you hire a consultant, they can help you out here a great deal. You'll find that small changes here and there can really save you money, but not affect your overall level of service.

If you are still unsure who will cover what duties at your spa, you can write up job descriptions for each position you are considering hiring. This will clarify your thinking, and make sure that you have staff to cover all required tasks. You can also use them as a basis to advertise the positions.

You can read a sample job description on the next page.

Sample Staffing Schedule

	Dry Massage Room	Mud Treatment Room	Esthetician Room	Wet Treatment Room
Thursday				
9:00 – 1:00	Julie	Janelle	Saul	Becca
1:00 – 5:00		Mark	Gwynn	Amanda
5:00 – 9:00	Benjamin	Ramin	Martina	

Sample Job Description

Spa Receptionist:

Reporting directly to the spa manager, the receptionist performs general reception and administrative duties, including answering phones and maintaining the client database.

Duties and responsibilities:

1. Answer spa phone in a professional, courteous manner.
2. Maintain client and personnel records for the spa.
3. Greet walk-in customers and those arriving for appointments in a professional, courteous manner.
4. Prepare reports on clients and personnel as needed.
5. Accept payments in cash, credit card and debit form from clients, and provide clients with appropriate receipt.
6. Answer general-question emails and forward others to spa manager.
7. Maintain policy and procedure database.
8. Work with spa manager in scheduling client appointments.
9. Provide a variety of supportive services as directed by the spa manager.
10. Performs other related duties as required.

Knowledge, skills and abilities:

1. Advanced knowledge of personal computers and multi-line phones.
2. Good analytical, organizational and problem-solving skills.
3. Knowledge of principles and practices of spa treatments.
4. Ability to communicate effectively both verbally and in writing with staff, employees and clients.
5. Ability to operate standard office equipment including photocopier, fax machine, and scanner.
6. Ability to follow both oral and written instructions.

4.6.2   Interviewing

More and more businesses are interviewing with a focus on asking about past behavior in order to determine what future behavior might be. Questions tend to start with "Tell me about a time when..." They are asking not about your philosophy or beliefs or what you would do in a hypothetical situation, but rather, what have you done in a specific situation in the past. With these types of questions you tend to get specific responses; not "this is what I would do" or "this is what I usually do" but "this is what I did do."

A similar interviewing style has a "trap" question before you ask a specific question about your past. An example might be: "Do you consider yourself a creative person?" If they say yes, you then ask, "Tell me about a time when you were creative." If they cannot think of a specific example, you'll want to consider this a questionable area of skill or talent.

You can also use negative questions to see if candidates can answer the questions positively. If you ask "What did you like least about your previous job?" there are many things a candidate might be tempted to complain about.

Any negative comment about a previous job or previous employer should make you wonder if they will have the same negative feelings towards you some day. A good answer will focus on what they did not have but are looking for, such as: "I am looking for an opportunity which gives me a chance for growth and development."

During the initial interview, take this opportunity to let the potential employee know what will be expected of him or her by going over a job description. If you are going to expect your staff to make a certain amount of retail sales per month, make this clear early on. Not all employees are comfortable with sales quotas, and should be given the option to back out of the hiring if this is the case.

What You Can and Can't Ask

It's important to know that there are some things that cannot be asked about in an interview. Some are simply illegal, and others are insulting and open the door to discrimination charges.

They are:

- Age

- Race

- Religion

- Marital Status

- Family Status or Pregnancy

- Disability

- Workers' Compensation Claims

- Injury

- Medical Condition

- Sexual Orientation

Selection Considerations

Be wary of candidates who:

- Bring up wage/salary and benefits questions too early

- Talk about "needing" rather than wanting the job

- Won't look you in the eye

- Use constricted body language

- Are "yes" people

- Are argumentative

- Try to control

- Don't listen

- Give you confusing answers

- Are not polite or nice to other applicants or staff

- Are not properly groomed

Select candidates who:

- Are polite

- Smile and make eye contact

- Are passionate about spa treatments

- Are enthusiastic

- Are tactful

- Are cheerful

- Have a good energy level

- Have a desire to help people

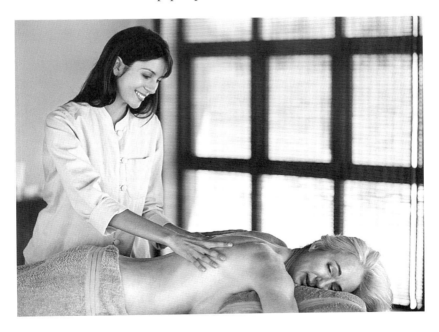

Spa Staff Interview Questions

Below are some sample interview questions, based on materials kindly supplied by spa industry experts Lori Hutchinson and Ann Brown, who developed a spa employment recruitment guide. You can use this form in an interview setting.

If I talked to your former/current supervisor, what would he/she say about your work?

_____

_____

_____

What have you done on your own to improve your professional skills?

_____

_____

_____

Why should we hire you?

_____

_____

_____

Name three trends in the industry today – please explain why you like or dislike each.

_____

_____

_____

Under what type of management style are you most productive?

_____

_____

_____

What do you know about this company?

_____

_____

_____

Describe an instance in which you went "beyond the call of duty."

_____

_____

_____

Where do you want to be five years from now?

_____

_____

_____

Describe your interpersonal style.

_____

_____

_____

Tell me ten adjectives that describe your personality at work.

_____

_____

_____

What creates stress for you? What do you do to eliminate stress?

_____

_____

_____

Tell me when one of your weak qualities caused a problem at work.

_____

_____

_____

4.6.3   What to Pay your Staff

Remember that there is no perfect way to pay your staff as a whole. You are going to have a mix of staff members with varying degrees of experience, many of whom perform vastly different tasks.

"It depends from spa to spa what formula of benefits, commissions, job status, etc. will work," says spa consultant Alexis Ufland. "There are pluses and minuses to each type of compensation, and the key is to find the right mix for your facility."

In this section we will outline some of the more common pay methods, but you will likely end up using a combination of them all. The best pay structure is the one that keeps your staff happy and productive, keeps turnover low and clients coming back, and keeps your margins where they need to be. Here are some options.

Salaried Wage

Paying your employees a set salary usually means more profitability for you, so long as you can nail down a number both parties are happy with. You must also take into account things like paying premiums to the government for workers' compensation, social security and Medicare. Salaries are generally offered to directors, managers, massage therapists and medical professionals only.

"We recommend calling the local massage schools and finding out what the average pay scales are," said Ufland. You can also use web based surveys and services such as Salary.com at **www.salary.com**. Here are some ballpark salary ranges for positions within the spa industry:

- *Spa Director:* Anywhere from just under $30,000 to more than $200,000

- *Assistant Director:* Anywhere from $25,000 to $65,000 a year, again depending upon their level of experience and the size and caliber of the spa at which they are working

- *Spa Manager:* Approximately $30,000 per year and up

- *Massage Therapist:* $40,000 per year and up; median base salary in the U.S. is $44,618 according to Salary.com

Hourly Rate

Most entry-level positions are paid hourly in a spa, and sometimes will include beginning massage therapists as well. Estheticians will likely prefer this option to commission only, especially when they are just getting started, as they are guaranteed a basic wage regardless of how many clients they deal with.

- *Spa Manager:* $16 to $20 per hour, depending on experience

- *Receptionist:* $10 to $13 per hour

- *Esthetician or Cosmetologist:* $8 to $15 per hour plus tips and commissions

Straight Commission

Paying by commission means that your staff are paid a percentage of the fee charged to each client they serve. Typical straight commission rates start at 50 or 60% of the cost of service, and range up to 70% for an experienced spa employee who supplies his or her own products. Again, the point is to find a percentage that works for both of you.

While having contractors instead of employees may seem like a great cost-cutting plan to reduce labor expense, and to motivate your staff to work hard, it can also be a scenario that backfires. First of all, it may be tough for you to attract talented staff when you are just launching your spa — they won't want to work for pennies while you grow the business, they want to step into hordes of paying clients.

When all your therapists and estheticians are on commission, you risk there being no sense of "team" in your spa. Staff may not want to promote each other's services as complementary, in case they lose a client to another staff member. When it works, commission is better suited to salon/spas, where this payment structure is the norm.

Hourly Plus Commission

In this scenario, employees agree to a combination of hourly wage and commission, both at a lower rate than if they were strictly one or the other. This gives the employee the chance to benefit from developing a loyal and consistent client base, but also allows a back-up for slow days, so employees don't have to wait around "on call". In these arrangements commission is closer to 30 or 40 percent, and the wage is reduced to the low end of the hourly samples listed above.

A similar form of compensation ties commission into the performance of all staff members, where they receive a base pay plus a commission that reflects the sales and service of the spa that month. Some spa owners find their employees have a better team attitude and more motivation when they are compensated using this structure.

Per Service

Once you have been in business for a while, you can use your financial data to break down an approximate cost to you for each service performed. You can then pay your employees a flat fee for each service, based on your desired margins.

Bonuses and Benefits

Offering health benefits, extra paid days off or occasional cash bonuses to your employees may cost you money, but they may also keep your employees loyal to your spa in a competitive market. Many business owners underestimate the cost of hiring and training new employees, and forget to factor in the lost revenue from losing an experienced employee and his or her satisfied clients.

Also, keep in mind that not all payment comes in the form of dollars and cents. You can think about ways you can make employees happy that cost relatively little, such as premium coffee in the break room, or an occasional after-hours staff party on your dime.

> **TIP:** Allowing your spa employees to bring guests in for free services from time to time benefits both of you. You get a new client, and your employee gets to brag about what they do, or trade for other services they want.

Jeremy McCarthy suggests that all spa staffers should experience different spa treatments (a nice "benefit") to understand what their guests go through. What does the floor feel like if you go barefoot in the steam room? What does it feel like to wear slippers that are not exactly your size? Having the experience of each spa service is an enjoyable perk for the employee, and helps them build empathy for the guests.

4.7 Your Grand Opening

The most exciting day you'll experience is your grand opening. All of the hard work and research has paid off. To ensure your day is all you imagined it to be, start planning several months in advance. Think of it like planning a wedding, or any other "grand" event.

One California spa owner we interviewed said she built her website six months before her grand opening. The site provided informational articles and a countdown to their grand opening that generated anticipation. Wow! You'll want to have a checklist of who you will contact and what you will do each week leading up to your opening.

Set aside time when you will pay your staff to come in and do a bit of training. It's not that they don't know how to do their jobs, but they need to know how to do it your way. You'll include this money in your start-up funding.

There are a few ways you can go about finding "guinea pigs" to get the bugs worked out of your system: you can start with friends and family, and once you are fairly confident, you can send out invitations to local merchants and business people.

You may spend a few thousand dollars doing this training, but you gain far more. Not only have you trained your employees well, but you engaged a lot of potential customers, pampered them, and made them feel that they are a part of your business.

There are many ways to make a grand opening a successful launch pad for your business — Chapter 6 will teach you what you need to know about sending press releases and spreading the word. In the meantime, check out this list of ideas shared with you by spa owners across North America.

- "Attend business or community events a few weeks before you open and hand out your business card to let people know to look for your business in the near future."

- "Hold a charity event for your grand opening. Charge a 'cover price' at the door, but make sure everyone knows the money will be donated to charity. Provide finger food and drinks, and give out small gift bags with your logo. Make sure you send out a press release announcing the charity event as your grand opening."

- "Print up inexpensive tickets that mimic theater tickets and hand them out to select individuals announcing an exclusive grand opening party. Serve upscale hors d'oeuvres and demonstrate mini spa treatments."

- "Hold a 50% off grand opening for friends and family only, to test your system and get feedback from supportive individuals."

- "Have a cyber-sweepstakes prior to your grand opening. When customers go to your website, ask them to register for a sweepstakes by providing their contact information. This generates excitement about your grand opening, and gives you a database of names to contact."

- "You can generate excitement about any upcoming event by writing a web log or 'blog.' Look at samples at www.blogger.com."

- "Have two grand openings: a private and true celebration with friends and family, and a professional event for the media and businesses. Make sure your staff knows who is designated to speak with the media and what they should say."

- "Place balloons with your logo outside of the spa and have an employee stand outside inviting people in to learn about services and treatments that your spa offers. Serve something light like wine and cheese, and have a small gift with your logo for them to take when they leave."

- "Send a letter to a local politician or media personality asking if she/he will come and say a few words at your event. Your best chance of getting their participation is to have a charity event."

- "Enjoy the day. You worked hard for this! Now is the time to shine."

5. Running Your Spa

As a consumer, your experience of a spa is that it is a beautiful and relaxing place. You may not be aware of the frenetic activity, long hours, and emotional investment percolating just under the surface to maintain that sense of nirvana for the sake of the customers.

5.1 Operations Systems

Make no mistake: you will need a number of systems in place to run your business. According to an article written by Alexis Ufland for About.com, 75% of complaints in a spa setting relate to what happens outside the spa rooms, which includes your reception area, taking appointments, your flow, your check out, etc.

Before you open the doors you want to have as many systems put in place as possible so everybody knows what they should be doing. You may think that it is enough to communicate your ideas by chatting with your director or staff, but there are far greater advantages to putting your systems down on paper.

Setting Your Hours of Operation

The hours of operation you choose should be specific to your location and clientele. If you are located in a 9 – 5 business area that becomes deserted at 5:05 p.m. every night, there's no point in staying open late. If you're located near movie theaters and night clubs, however, you may get some walk-by traffic interested in taking a menu with them.

Your hours will also depend on whether you are hiring a director, or if you are going to try to be onsite as much as possible yourself, as you should not spread yourself too thin. Once again this is an area where you will want to start cautiously. You can always add more hours, but you won't make any friends by reducing them.

Conventional spa hours are within the ranges of 9 a.m. to 9 p.m. Monday to Friday, and 9 a.m. to 7 p.m. Saturday and Sunday. 9 a.m. to 6 p.m. is also common Monday to Wednesday, and then open later Thursday and Friday leading up to the weekend. If you are in a mall or strip mall, your hours may be determined for you.

It is perfectly acceptable to close on Sunday if you desire, but of course you are losing potential business. You may want to try staying open every second Sunday at first, and see what the demand is in your area.

> **TIP:** Some spas choose to reserve evenings for private group bookings. This can be advertised along with your packages, and is popular with bridal parties or just for a girls' night out. You can read more about booking groups in section 5.4.4.

Whatever hours of operation you choose, make sure that you print them in your menu of services. Have a phone answering system that includes them as well in case someone calls after hours, and you can also direct people to your website, which of course is open 24 hours a day!

5.1.1 General Policies

You will want to develop and write out the following general policies related to the operation of your spa:

- *Job descriptions for each position:* Knowing what is expected of them is a major factor in employee satisfaction, according to a recently released study based on Gallup poll research.

- *Cleaning and maintenance schedule:* If staff is expected to perform routine maintenance on the equipment they use, they need to know this. If you hire someone or assign someone to this task, they need step-by-step instructions of what needs to be done, and how often, and have a chart they can fill in upon completion.

- *Procedures:* For day-to-day operations such as opening and closing cash registers, answering the phone, shutting down computers, lights to be left on, etc.

- *Troubleshooting manuals:* If you have to call a repair person every time something malfunctions, you are going to be paying out unnecessary money. Make a troubleshooting guide for each piece of spa equipment that is based on the manual that came with the machine. Add to it with every incident — so when someone says, "What did we do last time this happened?" you'll know.

- *Work schedules:* They don't need to have employee names yet, but you should know how many hours a week you want a massage therapist onsite, and how many of them at a time.

- *Company policies:* Do employees get sent home if things are slow? Do they get written up if they are late twice? What about three times? Do they have to purchase and wash their own smocks? These are the kinds of things your staff will resent not knowing if it comes as a surprise, so make a list that details your policies on these matters.

- *Record-keeping:* Do bills get filed away or tossed? How long are they kept for? Do you need to fill in all the information in the client information database, or is a name and phone number sufficient? Whoever maintains your filing systems (both electronic and paper) will need to know how you want your spa records kept.

- *Sales goals:* These will initially be based on your sales projections from your business plan, and eventually on last year's sales. You can post your progress to date for management to see, or everyone, so they can all feel involved.

- *Hierarchy:* "Make sure the staff knows the hierarchy and who reports to whom," Alexis Ufland told FabJob authors. Keeping everyone's roles clear from the beginning will make communication a lot easier during those critical early stages. Creating an organizational chart early on also makes it easier to understand new roles that get added once the business grows.

- *Safety and hygiene policies:* In most states the OSHA will require that you develop a plan for safe practices in the workplace, related to equipment, hygiene, etc. They will provide you the details of what they require. The website **www.oshafastfix.net** will sell you ready-made and custom materials to help you develop these.

Even if you spend a year designing and developing your new spa, plan on another year of operating glitches before you get all the bugs worked out. You will always be adapting to the changing needs of your business and your customer and always striving to be the best you can be.

5.1.2   Laundry

An important but not-so-glamorous aspect of running your spa is doing laundry. Spa owners caution that you don't underestimate the amount of laundry that will be used in just one week. It's devastating to business if you run out of fresh laundry, since you can't very well leave clients in the middle of a treatment room dripping wet without a towel.

There are really two key issues in managing laundry in a spa. The first is to determine what method of laundering is best for your spa: in-house, or outsourcing to a commercial service. Secondly, you'll need to arrange for an internal system of distribution that makes sure dirty towels are kept in a central place and never mixed with clean towels, and that clean towels are always at hand for both technicians and clients. Let's take a look at your options.

In-House Laundry

For many small and medium-sized spas, in-house laundry is the most cost-effective solution. With only detergent and the salary of the person responsible for laundry (usually a housekeeper), spa owners told us they cut their monthly laundry bill in half doing it in-house.

While in-house laundry can mean substantial savings, it also means a greater initial cost to the business, as you can expect to pay between $1,500 and $5,000 for a heavy-duty washer and dryer. And when the spa is dependent on the washer and dryer for all its linen needs, it's essential to purchase reliable, high-end machines.

You will also want to purchase a service contract with the manufacturer or dealer. While this is adding to the overall costs, it will give you peace of mind and you won't be faced with a big repair bill should one of your machines break down. If possible, have it written into the service contract how quickly a service person must show up — this might be anywhere from a few hours to a few days. This way you can keep a supply of clean towels at a level where you'll always have enough on hand to sustain a broken-down washer.

Another upfront cost with choosing in-house laundry is purchasing the towels and other textile linens. A bonus is that you will be able to choose them yourself, though, rather than renting whatever the commercial laundry service has available.

Outsourcing Laundry

While it's true that by outsourcing your entire laundry operation you may be limited in the choice of towels you use, many spa owners find the ease and convenience of a laundry service worth sacrificing a bit of style, and worth the extra monthly cost.

Jamie Lewis, general manager of Glacier House Resort and Alpine Meadow Spas, says that his operation decided to outsource their laundry for three main reasons: first, they did not want to introduce chemicals into their environmentally friendly system. Also, since commercial providers are experts in laundry, he felt that they could do a better job on his spa's linens than could be done in-house. The third reason was to help build business relationships within the community.

So how does a laundry service work? Commercial laundry services generally offer services in much the same way: a package includes laundry services, towel rental, and pick-up and delivery of laundry. What does vary, however, are the pricing models and contracts.

Most commercial laundries operate using either a price-per-unit or price-by-weight model. A price-per-unit model is based on the number of towels rented, and built into the price is the cost of pick-up, cleaning and delivery, which runs anywhere from 40 to 80 cents per towel per week, depending on the quality of the linen.

In a price-per-weight scenario, the cleaning service will weigh your towels at their facility, and bill you accordingly. Choosing a laundry service that charges by weight won't likely save your spa money, as their pricing is in line with those charging by the piece, but it may save you some time keeping track of pieces going in and out.

In most cases, outsourcing will mean a minimum monthly bill of several hundred dollars. Also, most laundry services insist on a long-term contract, most commonly between one and five years, so you will want to ask questions before you commit.

Towels and treatment-table linens can cause rashes or allergic reactions, so it's important when choosing a service provider to ask how they wash their laundry and what type of detergent they use. A good laundry service should be conscious of keeping pH levels in their wash water low, as a high pH level will produce calcium build-up on towels and linens.

Alsco is one of the largest laundry services, and they have specialized in hotels, spas and other wellness services for many years. There are also commercial laundry services across North America, servicing both cities and rural areas. See your local Yellow Pages for a commercial laundry service near you. To get a quote from Alsco, visit their website at **www.alsco.com** and call the office nearest to your spa.

Your Laundry Management System

The high volume of laundry handled in a spa means that an efficient system that keeps clean towels in the treatment rooms and soiled towels in the laundry is both a necessity and a challenge.

Regardless of how you choose to wash your laundry, you will need receptacles for soiled towels in each treatment room, and at least one large cart on wheels that can be moved around your spa with ease, as wet towels can be very heavy. Depending on the volume of clients, the laundry pick-up should be done, at the very least, at the end of each day. And the laundry person should try to restock a treatment room with the same number of towels that they remove.

Soiled laundry should be stored in an out-of-the-way place, away from clients' eyes. Your spa is a place for clients to escape from thinking about everyday life, and nobody likes being reminded of laundry.

If you choose to do laundry in-house, the best way to stay organized is to designate a laundry person, or hire a housekeeper. Having a designated person responsible for the laundry will help ensure that it's never left undone because someone forgot to do it, or decided not to do it. If you are planning on asking staff members to help out, make sure you make it clear at the interview that laundry is part of the job description, or you may be dealing with some bruised egos.

With outsourcing your laundry, and even for those doing in-house laundry, it's important to have an inventory system for your linens. An inventory count of what was sent to the laundry will help ensure that the service returns precisely what was sent out. It will also help you keep track of what's left in your spa, so you won't drop to a dangerously low level.

To do this, have a set amount of linens designated for each treatment room. At the end of each week, have the individual collecting the soiled laundry fill each treatment room with the set amount of clean linens, and collect the soiled ones. The number in the treatment rooms, plus those in the soiled basket, should add up to the total number of linens. For example, if you have 100 towels on site, and you have 10 towels in your five treatments rooms, then the soiled count should be 50.

You can use a laundry inventory sheet to track your totals. This sheet should hang in the laundry room and a new one should be filled out for each laundry period.

Sample Laundry Inventory Sheet

	Mud Room	Massage Room	Relaxation Room	Shower Room	Totals
Bath Towels	5	5	5	5	20
Hand Towels	5	5	5	5	20
Face Cloths	5	5	5	5	20
Clean Totals	15	15	15	15	60
Soiled Count	Date: _____				40
Clean and Soiled Count Combined	*(Overall count should equal 100)*				100

5.1.3   Maintenance and Housekeeping

Most spas are high-traffic environments with a high need for maintenance and housekeeping. There is equipment to clean, plenty of laundry to deal with, and a need for an immaculate environment to complete
the perfect experience for your guests.

As a spa owner you generally have a staff or team of people that can
help you with general cleanliness and basic maintenance and repairs,
but they may need direction from, you which means you have to go
through your spa with a highly critical eye.

Doing a Walkthrough

When you are in the spa every day there is a tendency to become overly
familiar with your environment. After a while, you no longer see things
with the critical eye necessary to find deficiencies in housekeeping
and maintenance. You want to make a frequent effort to see things
from the guests' point of view. Lie down on a massage table and see
what that experience is like. Does the table feel sturdy or does it rock
back and forth a little bit?

What do you hear? Does the table make any squeaking or creaking
noises? Can you hear the air conditioning? Can you hear an electric
buzzing sound from the lights? There are all kinds of ambient noises
in any spa facility that you would never notice in a normal day-to-day
routine. But in a very relaxed state when you are lying peacefully on a
massage table, even the smallest hum can be annoying.

How does the face cradle feel on your face? Are you comfortable? Do
the linens smell fresh and clean? Is there any lingering scent of
aromatherapy in the room? When you lie face down, what do you see?
Is there anything attractive on the floor to look at such as a bowl of
flowers or pebbles or a picture of some sort? Is the floor clean? Are the
therapist's shoes and feet clean and well manicured? (This may not seem
like it's your concern, but a client may be staring at them for 30 minutes
or more.)

If you are lying face up, there is plenty to evaluate also. Is the ceiling
pleasing and soothing to look at, or is it decorated with fire sprinklers
and emergency alarms and industrial-looking music speakers? Is the

ceiling clean? Are sprinkler heads and other features clean and free of rust?

Create a "punch list" of all of your housekeeping and maintenance items and check them off one by one as they are completed. The list is never finished — it should be an active document that grows and changes and expands as new items are needed.

General Cleaning

How important is keeping a clean spa? In short, it means everything. There are generally two main aspects of keeping a spa clean: general cleaning of the spa, and the cleaning and maintenance of equipment.

For general cleaning, most spas employ a full-time housekeeper, or contract a cleaning service. Some spa owners insist that having a house-keeper on staff produces better results, as the individual becomes part of the team, and takes pride and ownership in ensuring that the spa looks its best, but the choice is up to you.

The housekeeper is responsible for cleaning the entire spa, including the reception area, garbage, all the floors and, as noted, the laundry. The cleaning product used should be a mild disinfectant that has a light or neutral odor. You don't want the smell of artificial pine competing with the delicate fragrances and calming scents that you've chosen for your spa.

The general cleaning of a spa is not complicated, but it does require a great deal of attention, meaning that it must be done daily. It also requires numerous products and equipment. Here are some of the essentials:

- Broom/dustpan

- Cleaning brushes

- Cleaning cart

- Cleaning products

- Duster

- Mop/bucket

- Cloths

- Trolley laundry cart

- Washroom/shower cleaning equipment

You should occasionally go through the entire spa with guests' eye view to cleanliness as well. Sit in the chairs in your waiting area; go into the steam room. Look down into the drains of showers, and sit at the toilets in the changing area. (Many spas have separate employee restrooms, so you may be surprised to find out what your guests are looking at when they sit on the toilet in your guest restrooms.)

Maintenance of Spa Equipment

While the housekeeper is responsible for the general cleaning of the spa, the staff is ultimately responsible for the cleaning of the equipment that they use. The reason for this, says Norma Daniels, co-owner and spa director at High Fields Country Inn and Spa, is simply that technicians are familiar with the equipment — both how to use it and how to maintain it.

If you're a spa owner but not familiar with the hygiene and maintenance requirements of treatments tubs and other equipment, here are a few guidelines to ensure that your spa technicians are keeping this equipment clean and in working order.

All tubs, particularly those that are used for more than just water, such as mud baths, must be drained and cleaned with a manufacturer-recommended product after each treatment. This will prevent the spread of a contagious condition from client to client. At the end of each day the tub must not only be drained and cleaned, but the lines and spouts must be flushed with clean water.

Treatment tables can be disinfected daily by either the housekeeper or the staff who use them. Some technicians prefer to clean and maintain the tables themselves, while others will ask the housekeeper to perform this task.

Hygiene Issues

Until recently, the spa industry was largely self-regulated, with leading spa associations providing guidelines, inspections and certificates of approval. Today, however, state and provincial governments are taking a more active role in the development of guidelines and legislation, as well as inspections, which generally take place prior to opening and annually.

In many states and provinces this transition is still under way. You can contact your national spa association (listed in section 2.3.4) to help you determine which health authority is responsible for governing spa and wellness centers in your area.

Your massage technicians and estheticians will be trained in the rules governing their trade, which include techniques for cleaning reusable equipment, and not "double-dipping" back into product. They may also be required to have training in disease transmission prevention.

The best way to educate yourself on hygiene requirements is to become a licensed cosmetologist or esthetician, and perhaps you are. If not, you should sit down with your director, manager and/or staff and make a list of what rules need to be observed.

Your vendors will also be able to educate you and your staff on how to handle their equipment and products safely. Your staff are the ones who've been trained, but you will be the one liable for any slip-ups, so this is not an area to ignore, or assume that it is being done correctly.

5.2 Managing your Team

The spa business is a "people" business in more ways than one. You not only have to pamper and please your customers, you also have to lead your team of employees. Spa employees by nature tend to be a little more sensitive and therefore respond well to leadership that also shows a great deal of sensitivity.

So how do you motivate your staff to be the best they can be? Here are some ideas on communicating with spa people and keeping them happy and productive.

5.2.1   The Importance of Staff Relations

Remember that you are offering a luxury service, and your staff needs to be super-attentive to their client's needs and wants. The basic mindset is that if your client is going to spend money on "pampering" themselves, they need to feel that they have truly had their needs met in a professional and friendly way.

If your staff members are grumbling and unhappy, or even somewhat stand-offish, your clients will find somewhere else to go. They may even think that the staff is judging them, their body, their lifestyle choices, etc., simply because they are not approachable, or having a bad day. Friendly staff puts clients at ease, and make them feel comfortable in an intimate setting where they are exposing their privacy.

Because massage therapists in particular use their sensitivity to perform their job, it is important that they have the opportunity to express anything which might be affecting how they feel. Getting their feelings and thoughts out on the table helps them to be clear-headed and "tuned in" when they are with their guests.

Your employees also have a great deal of information about your customers and their likes and dislikes. Most are very respectful of their guests' privacy, so it's possible that a lot of great information that could be used to improve your operation never goes beyond the treatment room. Ask your employees to share information that could help improve your customers' satisfaction.

5.2.2   Communication with Spa "People"

Spa employees in general are a little more holistic and spiritual, which makes them great at what they do in the spa. But that free-spirited nature also makes it more challenging to bring them together as a team and get them to buy in to your business objectives.

Toni Howard, a veteran spa manager, told one of our authors an interesting story about a busy morning in the spa when she answered a call from one of her therapists:

> "Toni, things have been going wrong for me all morning and so I checked, and guess what? Mercury is in retrograde! I really don't

think it is a good idea for me to come into work today." Howard suppressed her panic as she surveyed the full schedule for the spa that day.

"I don't care if the Earth is about to collide with the Sun," Toni said quietly but firmly, "If you ever want to come in again, you will get here for your first appointment!" In spite of all the astrological forces working against her, the therapist made it in.

The truth is, there are few of us who are giving enough, sensitive enough and caring enough to devote our lives to healing other people by laying our hands on them. We should count ourselves lucky that such wonderful people are out there, and willing to work in your spa.

Most employees in any setting generally appreciate one-on-one conversations or small intimate groups with plenty of opportunities to express their feelings on different subjects, and spas are no exception. Small meetings or focus groups are a great way to generate new ideas and get input on new strategies for the spa. It is also an ideal time to air out any misunderstandings or sources of tension that may have formed within the group.

Especially since so much of spa employees' work takes place behind closed doors, taking a moment to share some positive feedback from a guest or to thank them for doing a great job goes a long way.

5.2.3   Inspiring and Motivating

How do you get people excited? How do you get them motivated? How do you get efficient use of time and resources?

Spa professionals live and breathe their work, so they often appreciate the "psychic rewards" of their work more than the monetary compensation. Jonathan Stapleton, General Manager of the Old Course Hotel, Golf Resort & Spa in Scotland said, "I haven't yet met a therapist who didn't deeply and genuinely believe in the transformational power of their work and care passionately about it. That quality alone is so rare in today's working environment."

Spa owners should appreciate and encourage this quality in their staff. By virtue of the beliefs they hold, massage therapists are highly motivated employees. This is one case where the employee has more interest in the results of their work than the manager does.

David Erlich, Director of Spa Operations for the Fairmont Sonoma Mission Inn and Spa, says that spa employees "give so much of themselves for a living, that a good manager must recognize when they need to receive as well," said Erlich.

Think about giving your employees the opportunity to trade with their co-workers and experience the treatments themselves. Not only do they appreciate this form of motivation, but it helps them to learn from their peers and to understand the whole process better from a client's point of view.

"Due to the caring nature of their personalities," adds Jonathan Stapleton, "they often don't take time for themselves." The manager should recognize this and, when appropriate, encourage them to take some time out for a treatment, a stretch or some quiet relaxation.

As in any business, employees like to be kept in the loop with what's going on with the business, so they feel engaged and appreciated. Try to find the time to schedule meetings that are just about the spa's progress in general, or type out a one-page staff newsletter that details plans and ideas you are thinking about putting into place. Extend an invitation for feedback as well.

You should also schedule regular performance reviews, which can be held informally over coffee, or in your office. Staff need to know that what they are doing (good and bad) is being noticed, and a face-to-face meeting can really clear the air. Sometimes managers will "forget" these meetings in an attempt to avoid giving staff raises… but rest assured that the staffer didn't forget, and will be looking for another employer in the meantime.

5.3   Retail Sales

Most spas sell retail products to boost their profitability, and day spas in particular can make a lucrative business from retail. You may even plan to have a dedicated retail space to sell products from, or just a few shelves in the lounge area, so long as it matches your spa concept and available space.

We say that day spas "can make" a good profit from retail, but not all spas do. In order to boost your retail sales, you need to get your whole staff on board with the program. This isn't always easy, since the people who work in a spa are not trained salespeople, they are trained spa professionals. You can help them feel better about selling to clients by paying for them to take sales courses, and by having excellent products for sale that they can feel confident recommending.

Preston Inc. Spa Consulting has an excellent article online about helping your staff ease into the role of super salesperson. You can read the article, titled "My Employees Won't Sell Retail Products!" at **www. psbsolutions.net/Knowledge-Base-Login/Articles/Retail-Service-Sales/My-Employees-Won-t-Sell-Retail-Products!-Why-this-.aspx** (Free sign-up required)

5.3.1   What to Sell

Any retail manager strives to find that perfect combination of products and merchandise that will sell well and meet the needs of their clients. This is an elusive goal, and both the displays and the products need to be updated frequently to reflect changing trends, changing seasons or changing clientele.

Most importantly, you should sell products that complement your spa. Every item available should make sense with your image. For example, Royal Paws Resort and Day Spa has a gift store that sells Egyptian cotton monogrammed bath towels — for dogs.

There are companies who will label bottled water or sparkling cider with your spa's name for clients to take away with them. Some luxury spas will sell spa supplies like robes and towels, or printed t-shirts and other branded merchandise.

The obvious product to sell is the line of skin care products used in your spa. If you choose to affiliate yourself with a particular brand, they may want you to enter into an exclusivity agreement with them where you sell only their product. This is fine so long as they give you a fair price, and their line of products is broad enough to appeal to a range of clientele.

Selling private-label products (skin care products made and packaged specifically for your spa) is also popular in day spas, since you can accomplish the double goals of generating revenue and putting your name into the minds and memories of your clients.

You stand a better chance of earning the business of a loyal client if you can offer them value they can take home with them — and only buy at your spa. You can usually make a good profit on private label products, too, since they are generally less expensive for you to buy than brand-names, but most people are willing to pay the same.

> **TIP:** The common industry commission that kicks back to estheticians for referring a client to a product that they make a retail purchase of is 10 to 20 percent.

You may also choose to complement your skin care products with other wellness items such as aromatherapy oils, candles, books on diet and meditation, etc. If you visit the websites listed at the end of this book, you will find a wealth of products for your consideration.

5.3.2 Pricing and Inventory

You will need to have systems in place to track the sales of your retail products. Many spa software packages offer this feature, and allow you to generate SKUs and price tags, as well as print out an up-to-date inventory at any time. We list some of the spa software you can choose from at the end of this guide.

If you sell only a few products, whoever you have selling the products can take a manual inventory once or twice a week, after which you can place an order. Your vendors will probably also be happy to provide you with order sheets that double as inventory sheets, and will call you to see how sales are going.

When you sell retail products in a spa environment, you want to keep the average cost of goods sold to 40 percent or less. That means that if you buy an item or product from the wholesaler for $20, you will sell it for at least $50.

Another way this is expressed is as markup, and you will hear of a standard markup of in retail of 100 percent: this means that you sell for double the price you paid, or with a 50% cost of goods sold. This is suitable when you sell a lot of product, but in a spa environment, the retail is secondary to the service.

It is okay if your cost of goods sold is higher for some items and lower on others, so long as the average is below 40%. In fact, private label products, which can be cheaper for you to purchase, can be marked up to 200% or higher, and still blend in with the prices of your other products.

> **TIP:** Don't forget to factor commissions into your mark-up price. If you charge a higher markup, you can pass that amount along to your employees in commission, and they will in turn be motivated to attempt to sell more products.

5.3.3 Displaying Your Products

Depending on the size and focus of your spa, you may have an entire area dedicated to retail sales. For example, Carapan Urban Spa is a Southwestern-themed day spa in the heart of the West Village in New York City.

Spas are at a premium in the Big Apple and competition is fierce, yet Carapan remains a popular choice for celebrities and neighborhood spa junkies by offering a total spa experience from the moment they step inside the retail store. With incense burning, Native American chants playing and dream catchers swaying from the ceiling, Carapan invites the spa-goer to enjoy the environment and shop the hundreds of products artfully placed throughout the store.

Making sure your product is placed in a way that invites interest is the formula for great sales. One spa owner told us she makes it easy for customers to explore on their own by color-coding the products with a dot representing formulas for oily, dry and combination skin. She finds her customers enjoy touching the testers and reading the ingredients. She makes it convenient for them to find exactly what they need.

Another spa owner says she trains her estheticians and massage therapists to expertly sell during the services to ensure the customer is getting the best product for their needs and to limit returns and dissatisfaction with product.

TIP: Consider placing small add-on products near the reception area. A new nail polish color or travel sizes of new shampoos sell easily as the customer prepares to pay for his or her service.

5.4 Day-to-Day Operations

Here is a look at some of the common daily operations in your spa, and tips for making all these areas of your business contribute to your profitability.

5.4.1 Booking Appointments

If business is going well, most of your calls will be about scheduling an appointment to enjoy one of the spa's treatment offerings. Your receptionist will help the caller schedule a mutually convenient time.

He or she can also be instructed to inform clients of monthly specials and new services. They should explain the benefits of the new treatment and why they think the client will enjoy it. If the client tries and likes the new service, he's likely to tell others about the experience, and next time will book the "usual" in addition to the new service you've introduced him to.

As owner you may occasionally answer the phone or help someone wishing to schedule an appointment, especially when you first start up. Ultimately, your goal is to have a staff of people that perform this function, but you will be setting the pace for them by your training, feedback and evaluation, and modeling. Your voice should instill a spa feeling. Keep it soothing and calming.

One of the secrets of a successful spa is that they manage to hide the administrative aspects from the customers. People come to a spa to have a retreat from their office environment. They do not want to experience ringing phones and messy stacks of paperwork when they come to the spa, as this will only serve to remind them of their hectic week at work.

A good owner can train their staff to efficiently and calmly answer several phone calls, sometimes simultaneously, on multi-line phones, and can efficiently and neatly process all of the paperwork necessary to the day-to-day operation.

When you and your staff are scheduling appointments, remember to keep in mind the unique nature of certain spa treatments, which may require time afterwards to shower, or simply to relax and come back to awareness.

The receptionist can also let new clients know at the time of booking if their treatment requires them to arrive early, or you can simply ask all clients to arrive 15 minutes ahead of their scheduled appointment time to allow a few moments to enter "spa mode".

Spa Software

You will also need to have systems in place for efficient appointment tracking, so that the spa does not become overbooked in either therapists or treatment areas. You want appointments to be as easy to make as possible with little or no room for error.

Again, this may involve use of one of the many spa software packages out on the market. Yes, even the sacred walls of the spas have been invaded by technology. As the saying goes, necessity is the mother of invention, and as spas have grown busier and busier, the need for software to computerize and control the business has grown as well.

Computer systems help to ensure that rooms and therapists are not accidentally overbooked. They keep track of which therapists are authorized to do which treatment and in which room. They can run reports to show you what your business is doing. And they can be your point-of-sale system for billing and controlling the inventory of your retail products.

If you know how to use any computer program, chances are you can learn another if it is not too complicated. The more fluent you become, the more productive you will be. The important thing to consider in any system is whether it works for you and your spa. See how the bonus features integrate into the rest of your spa.

> **TIP:** You can take a day or half a day comparing the demo versions of these software packages, which you can often download for free off the company website. Take note of the user-friendly features, as well as the overall usefulness of the software.

Sample Client Booking Schedule

	Dry Massage Room (J. Smith)	Mud Treatment Room (D. Black)	Esthetician Room (S. Sharma)	Wet Treatment Room (T. Ross)
Monday				
8:30 a.m.	Alice Brown	Jamie Jones	John Good	Roberta Hay
9:00 a.m.	Laura Smith	Nigel Ahan	Rebecca Court	Brian Reading
9:30 a.m.	Amir Kajan	Teresa Gee	Sharee White	Celia Johnson
10:00 a.m.	Linda Roberts	Roger Hume	Tracey Daniels	Valencia Wright

Above is a simplified version of what your booking sheets or appointment software will look like.

5.4.2   Greeting Clients

Once the client arrives for their appointment they will be greeted and checked into the system. It's best to try to schedule your appointments and use your treatment rooms in such a way that the client has little or no wait, unless you offer amenities during the wait that make it more pleasant.

> **TIP:**   This block of time may be your spa's only true opportunity to stand out from the competition, especially if you will offer similar services. Make it truly pampering, creative, and unique.

The spa experience is meant to be relaxing one, so it is of the utmost importance that the guest has no doubts or anxiety about where they should go or what they should be doing. As much as possible, the staff should take them by the hand and lead them through the experience so they feel completely taken care of.

A typical sequence might have a guest arriving for his appointment, checking in or signing in before being escorted to a change room where a robe and slippers await him in a locker. Other amenities and facilities such as showers, saunas and steam rooms might be available at this time.

Just before their appointment they are directed or escorted to a relaxing area where they await being picked up by their therapist, esthetician, or body treatment specialist. If you don't plan on having a relaxing room or change rooms, the client can also be led directly to the treatment room and can change and wait for their spa experience there. If it's the guest's first visit to the spa, have them fill out a client questionnaire such as the sample shown in section 4.4.3 of this book.

You will need to create procedures for receptionists and other staff to ensure that this process is as easy and stress-free as possible. Sometimes you might even act as expediter, ensuring that all guests have arrived and keeping an eye on them until they are safely in the hands of their therapist.

5.4.3   Payments and Checkout

After enjoying the spa services, the customer will need to settle their account at the reception desk. This should be handled professionally, and as quickly as the client desires.

You'll have to decide in advance what form of payment you want to accept, but the standards to offer are cash, debit, or major credit card. Personal checks may be more common if you live in a small town or close-knit community, but it will be hard to have one policy for locals and one for "out-of-towners," so you may want to not take checks at all. (It also makes for more paperwork and more frequent trips to the bank.)

If you want to accept credit cards, you'll need to set up a merchant account. To accept Visa or MasterCard, you may have to work with a bank to get an account set up and get the necessary point-of-sale equipment and supplies. Discover and American Express set up merchant accounts nationally and internationally without the requirement of working with a local institution.

You can also accept debit cards, which deduct payment directly from your client's bank account and deposits it into your business account. Be sure to mention to your equipment supplier that you would like to program the machine to prompt the client for a tip.

You should know that being able to accept credit cards comes with a price. You'll pay either a percentage of every credit card payment or a monthly fee, depending on what arrangements you make. Not a payment you enjoy making, but it's a service that clients have come to expect.

Having the client up and paying for services is an opportunity to sell them a bit more too, since they are hopefully relaxed, rejuvenated and in a great mood. There are diverse opinions about how to handle these last-minute sales, especially of retail products.

Some spas will bring the products used in the treatment right up to the counter, while others will have the employee doing the treatment feel the client out a bit, and see how open they are to buying first.

This last-minute push for business is either going to be perceived as an unnecessary intrusion, or a helpful hand, and most of this perception will be based on how comfortably your employee handled product suggestion during the treatment. Again, sales courses and having an excellent product will help.

It is always a nice idea to invite the client to book a future spa appointment at that time. Spa treatments are something that many people enjoy scheduling in advance, to make sure they aren't missed. Massages can be enjoyed anytime, and facials and body treatments become necessary again as their effects wear off. And of course, salon visits, if you offer that service, are needed as frequently as monthly to maintain a short stylish coif.

If they prefer not to schedule on the spot, you can send them a reminder by mail (this can be a thank-you card for first-time guests) in a few weeks. Your spa software should be able to track appointments and keep up with any clients who don't rebook.

Spa Gift Certificates

Gift certificates are much more of a commodity in the spa industry than in other types of businesses, as a trip to the spa is a fairly universally appreciated gift, particularly among women. You will sell many of these around special holidays such as Valentine's Day and Mother's Day, the winter holidays, and year-round as birthday gifts.

Make your gift certificates attractive and reflective of your spa. A good business printing company will have many creative ideas for creating a gift certificate package that is attractive and unique.

You will want to make sure that your gift certificates are prominently displayed at your checkout area, and that they are mentioned in your menu, your website, and any promotional materials you have printed. Prepare a package that you distribute with gift certificates (this can be your menu or an adaptation of it) that will help the recipient choose a service.

In a spa setting you can have gift certificates for monetary amounts as well as for specific services, such as a massage. Offering gift certificates for services allows people to give a gift "without a price tag". As the prices for services may fluctuate, make sure that there is an expiration date on the service-specific certificate, such as six months or one year.

If you plan to make your gift certificates non-refundable (many spas do) you should state this on the gift certificate, as well as the receipt. If you have a client who is adamant that they would not use a spa service and wants a refund, you can offer them an equivalent value of product to take home instead. In the end, it may save you grief (and a scene in your reception area) by refunding the occasional gift certificate to an irrational client, but you can generally come to some kind of an agreement.

Finally, remember that everyone loves gift certificates, and they are a great way to trade services with other retailers or service providers, or get some publicity at a reduced cost. You can contact the local mall and give them a gift certificate to raffle off (great publicity), or exchange gift certificates with complementary businesses such as a yoga studio. You can in turn use the received gift certificate to reward your staff members as you see fit.

Accepting Tips

Tipping is a regular practice at a spa, and some spas or salons like to offer the option of tipping privately, in a separate envelope that you write your caregiver's name on. Again, this is one of the many ways you can make your clients feel like their privacy is being respected in your environment.

Some spa owners will add a tip of 15 to 20 percent into the cost of the service, and call it a service fee. If this is the case, you should mention in your spa menu that your service providers' tips are included in the menu prices.

To avoid confusion, you can also mention in your spa menu if they are not, and suggest an appropriate range, or tell them that their recommendation to friends is their greatest gift.

5.4.4   Accommodating Groups

Being able to accommodate large groups in the spa is good for business. There is less work involved on a per-client basis (you might book 10 appointments with just one fax, email or phone call) and since they are often not spending their own money, they are generally easier to please. It is much easier to exceed someone's expectations when they are enjoying the service for free!

The other obvious advantage is that it gets people into your spa who might not normally use spa services. If you treat them right, you just may end up with a customer for life.

There are many different types of groups, and not all of them have the company footing the bill, but generally speaking, having a large group of clients who want to come to the spa is always a good thing.

The best kind of groups are "incentive" groups, usually comprised of a sales team who are being rewarded for achieving their goals by a trip to your spa. Other groups that may come to the spa include executive board meetings, educational seminars, association meetings, and special events such as weddings, family reunions, birthday parties, etc.

Booking the Services

You or your spa director will want to get personally involved with group bookings, to ensure everything goes smoothly.

This means contacting them early on in the planning stage and giving them all of the information and options they need to make their decisions. As much as possible, you also want to book group appointments in off-peak times, leaving other times available for non-group guests. This may include evenings or weekends when you would normally be closed.

If a large group wants to book the whole spa privately, expect them to ask you how many appointments the spa can accommodate per hour. It is better not to give this information upfront, especially if you are a small spa, since they may decide on their own you can't handle their numbers.

Instead, ask them how many appointments they need and then prepare some suggested schedules to accommodate those needs in the way that works best for the spa. You can arrange to move people through the spa in a way that doesn't congest the treatment rooms, using some advance planning.

In a spa that caters to groups, it might be a good idea to have a lot of treatment options available in the same price range. For example, if a one-hour massage, a facial and a manicure/pedicure all cost the same, then a group can offer a lot of options to their participants while knowing that the dollar value is the same for everyone.

It is important to have a signed contract or some type of written communication with the group, which clearly explains your cancellation policy and fees. Usually groups are locked into their appointments within 24 to 48 hours of the scheduled times. Some spas have cancellation windows that extend out to seven days or even a month before, sometimes with tiered cancellation fees that get higher as the date approaches.

A sample contract for group bookings appears on the next page.

Sample Contract for Group Bookings

In signing this contract, I, _____, agree to be the representative for the group (_____) that has rented the spa on _____, from _____ a.m./p.m. to _____ a.m./p.m. I will ensure that this group adheres to the following policies and procedures.

1. All individuals who are using the spa for the first time will fill out a medical and new-customer questionnaire.

2. Cancellation of this booking in whole or in part must be done a full 48 hours prior to the booking date. Failure to do so will result in the group being charged in full, without services.

3. All group members will stay no longer than one session for any treatment.

4. All group members will observe the no-smoking policy.

5. The group will agree to pay the full group rate upon arrival at the spa.

6. All group members will arrive on time, or agree to pay an extra treatment fee as a late charge.

7. All group members agree to conduct themselves in a manner that is appropriate to the spa environment.

8. All group members will observe the no-alcohol policy.

[Insert description of services to be provided]

[Insert statement of fees]

_____   _____

Signature   Date

5.4.5   Handling Complaints

Complaints are an inevitable part of doing business — you can't please everybody, but you can do your best to try. Especially when you first open, new reception and treatment staff make complaints more likely. Even down the road, something as simple as the supplier sending you a slightly different fragranced product can have a negative effect on your business.

Sample Letter of Apology

[Company Logo – Letterhead]

Dear Mrs. Jones,

On behalf of Splendid Spas, I've taken the time to write this formal letter of apology. At Splendid Spas we strive to give our clients the best spa experience possible. With this in mind, I would like to take this opportunity to tell you how truly sorry we are concerning your recent negative experience with us.

Based on your complaint, we have examined and rectified the situation. We are so confident that this issue has been resolved to your satisfaction that we would like to offer you a free massage on any day of your choice. Simply phone our spa and book an appointment. Then, bring this letter in with you to receive your free massage.

Again, we apologize for not meeting both our high standards and yours. We do hope to serve you again, and we are confident that your next experience at Splendid spas will be the enjoyable experience it is intended to be.

Sincerely,

[Your Name],
Owner

One of the best solutions is that you be available personally to handle complaints. If you were not in the spa when the incident occurred, you can follow up with a phone call later, if possible.

When receiving the complaint, listen attentively, and make sure you understand what is being said. Even if the customer is excited or irrational, remain professional and listen to what they have to say. Express your apologies, and if appropriate, bring it up at the next staff meeting if changes need to be made.

Depending on the complaint, you may want to follow up with a phone call or personal letter at a later time to explain how you have made changes to rectify the situation, and offer a free spa visit or reduced price to the disgruntled client to come back again. A sample letter of apology appears on the facing page.

5.5   Financial Performance

As owner you will want to closely monitor the financial performance of your spa. The more you know your numbers and the better you are at reacting to them, the better business you will run. This doesn't mean that you have to balance the books by yourself, but an owner who doesn't take an interest in profit margins and budgeting is a recipe for disaster.

5.5.1   Sales Goals and Budgeting

A budget is a financial plan for how the business will go over the course of the year. The budget contains an estimate of the revenues that the spa will earn, the expenses that will need to be paid out to make those revenues, and the "bottom line" or profitability of the spa.

- Spa revenues are the monies coming into the spa when your customers pay for goods and services.

- Cost of sales represents what you pay out for the goods and services you are selling.

- Labor costs are what you pay out to the people who are working to sell and provide your goods and services.

• Other expenses covers everything else that drains money out of your spa, from the pencils at your reception desk to the toilet paper in your client washroom.

Put simply, the budget shows these values:

    Total Spa Revenues
    –   Cost of Sales
    –   Labor Costs
    –   Other Expenses
        - - - - - - - - - - - -
    =   Spa Profit

If you have ever seen a budget on paper, though, you know that it is slightly more complicated than four numbers summed up for the profit total. The numbers are usually broken down for each month over the course of the year, with totals at the end.

Each number is further broken down into line items so that "Spa Revenues" becomes broken down into "Massage Revenue," "Facial Revenue," "Body Treatment Revenue," and "Retail Revenue" and so on.

TIP: While spa services may or may not be taxable in your region, retail sales are always taxable, so keep your income statements categorized by type of income.

Part of preparing your business plan will involve drafting operating budgets for your business. Use your budget as a benchmark, and refer to it as frequently as daily in your first month of operation, weekly in your first year, and monthly once your business is more settled and predictable.

It may be tempting to put off comparing your budget to actual figures, especially when simply running the business is so consuming, but you have to make the time to get this done. Sit down with your accountant or director and have them explain little things to you line by line, as well as their impression of the big picture.

A successful business responds to drops in revenue or increases in expenses as they happen, by shortening staff shifts temporarily, holding a promotional sale, stepping up advertising, or altering retail prices. It does you no good to find out three months later that you have been selling a product at the wrong price, or that a particular spa service is costing you way more than you are making on it.

Setting Sales Goals

The profit and loss (P&L) statement is one of the most important financial reports of a spa, and should be evaluated each month (or even more often) to see how well you are doing compared to your budget and where you might need to exert your efforts to improve the profitability of your spa.

The profit and loss statement shows the actual performance of your spa compared to the budget for one particular month. This report is usually created each month to give you a snapshot of how you have done that month, and where you are year-to-date compared to your budget for the year.

If you are making more profit than your business had budgeted, congratulations, and keep up the good work! If your profit is not as high as was expected, some kind of action will need to be taken.

5.5.2 Responding to the Numbers

Here are some examples of how your financial reports might reflect a certain problem that needs to be addressed with different strategies.

1. Revenues do not meet budget

If revenues are not meeting budget, efforts need to be made to either get more people to come into your spa, or get the people who come into your spa to spend more money. The former can be accomplished through marketing campaigns, public relations, promotions, special events, etc. They latter may require different strategies such as price increases, up-selling, retail selling, offering add-on services and activities, etc.

2. Cost of sales is too high

If the cost of sales is too high, it may mean you need to put some controls in place to limit the cost of the products in the treatments. Or, you might look at changing some of your retail selection to something with a higher profit margin.

In other words, if you buy a lotion for $15 and sell it for $20, your cost of sales is 75%. If you find a lotion that costs you $10 that you could sell for $20, you would cut your cost of sales considerably, to 50%.

3. Labor cost is too high

If you have more people working than what was budgeted, your labor costs will be cutting into your profitability. Sometimes extra efforts can be made to reduce this number by letting staff go when they are not needed, sending people on vacations and extra days off during slow periods, and so on.

Sometimes, however, you just need more people than the budget allows to get the job done. Hopefully that increased labor will affect the bottom line, and you can justify that increasing the labor cost will also help to increase revenues or reduce other expenses, so that the profitability target, the most important number, can still be met.

4. Expenses are too high

If expenses are too high, it might require some digging to find out why that is. The P&L usually breaks expenses out into line items so you can see what you spent money on. Maybe you had new spa menus printed and so your "Printing and Stationery" line was over budget. Perhaps the fresh cut gardenias in your waiting room are getting too expensive in your "Decoration" line.

Spa Gregorie's – A Study in Success

Angela Courtwright opened her own spa in Newport Beach, California, in the fall of 1998. She left behind a lucrative 20-year career as a marketing executive to pursue her dream of opening a spa. "I had absolutely zero spa experience," said Courtwright, "but a heck of a lot of business sense."

Courtwright was drawn to the spa industry after battling burnout in her high-stress job. "I was the poster child for 'Type A' stress," she said. "I was unhealthy and whacked out." She would go to spas a couple of times a month to restore her sense of normalcy and bring a little peace to her crazy life.

Those visits spawned her decision to switch industries, and when her software company merged with Time Warner, it gave her the financial windfall she needed to pursue her goal. "With the help of friends in the industry we created a business model that looked doable to me," she says. So she did it.

Courtwright began to research the industry fervently, reading every book, resource and trade magazine she could get her hands on. She was gifted with a clear vision of what her spa should be, and a keen eye for design and décor. Working with architects who could help her on the operational nuts and bolts of the project, she was able to create something special. "You don't have to have a lot of talent in everything," she counseled, "but you have to have a clear vision of what you want your spa to be and how the experience you offer will be distinct."

Courtwright used consultants to guide her vision, but went her own way when she disagreed with the consultants' advice. For example, when she decided to make her treatment rooms smaller to fit one more in, she was told it was "suicide". She stuck to her guns (at 10'x12', the rooms were still ample for her services), and the additional room has brought in a ton of additional revenue.

Since she launched her spa in 1998, Spa Gregorie's has shown double-digit growth almost every year, and is on its third expansion. Courtwright's spa has no more room to grow unless she opens a second spa in a new location. "With these kinds of numbers," said Courtwright, "if we were a public company we would be the number-one stock on the New York Stock Exchange!"

For Angela Courtwright, the best reward is knowing that her customers leave feeling better than they did when they arrived. Being successful allows her to give even more and get involved in community work and the spa is a perfect vehicle with which to make a difference.

Angela shared the following insider advice for new spa owners:

- Hire people with the right mindset, heart and philosophy who share your work ethic. Not only will they help you succeed, you will enjoy your life much more.

- Figure out the most motivating compensation structure for your team. Do not assume they want what you would want.

- If you do not have strong management and leadership skills, then hire someone who does. You need someone who can rally your troops.

- When forecasting your first-year budget, overestimate how long it will take your business to ramp up.

- Start small, but leave yourself room to grow.

- Be sure you have enough capital. It is very easy to underestimate what you need.

- Use the industry conferences and publications, and talk to other people in the industry. This can save you a ton of heartache and money learning from what others have already learned.

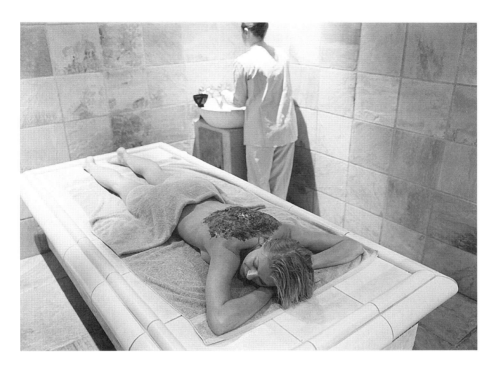

6. Getting Clients

"Many spa owners lack a solid brand identity. They miss out on unique marketing messages — there is no marketing budget or plan, no retail opportunities, and they underutilize the web as a vehicle for growth."

— *Joan Komorowski, featured speaker,*
  Spa & Resort Expo/Medical Expo

We design a beautiful setting, create a peaceful ambience, and dream up a delicious menu of treatments... why is this not enough? Because there are thousands of spas out there, most of which have beautiful décor and interesting, creative treatment menus with unique products.

Getting clients involves putting out an effort to attract new people to your spa, impressing them with top-notch service while they're there, and then keeping your spa in people's minds one month, three months, and even years down the road.

Here are some conventional and unconventional ways to attract and keep the lifeblood of your spa business: your clients.

6.1 Promotional Tools

Getting the word out about your spa is not hard with the abundance of promotional tools available. From websites to business cards to brochures, it's easy to get a professional printer or website design firm to create something that says, "Here we are!"

But to be successful, you need to say more than come book services "because we're here." Use your promotional tools listed below to your full advantage, and make them speak for you.

6.1.1 Your Website

We mentioned earlier that one spa owner told us she had her website designed six months before her grand opening, to introduce the local area to their spa and to generate pre-opening excitement.

It's not possible in today's market to overvalue what your website can do for business. However, it's also important not to expect your website to be some kind of "magic pill" that brings clients streaming through your doors, so treat it like it is — one very important component of an overall marketing approach.

What to Include

Your spa's website should include:

- Your logo

- Your spa's location (a small map helps)

- Your phone number

- Your hours of operation

- An email address to contact

- Your mission statement

- A brief description of the ambiance of your facility

- Your menu of services

- Accepted methods of payment

- Spa etiquette and policies

- A way to collect email addresses and phone numbers to add to your client database

You may also choose to add some of the following features:

- A way to buy spa products or gift certificates online

- Monthly specials

- A virtual tour video

- Information about the products you use

- Photos of treatment rooms and relaxation lounge, and surroundings if beautiful

- Testimonials from happy and/or celebrity clients

- Profiles of you and your best employees

- Skin care and wellness advice

- A careers/jobs page

Remember to make your website consistent with the image of your spa. Don't underestimate the power of words, colors and images to take your potential client "virtually" into your environment.

> TIP: If you have a recognizable private label skin care or bath line, you may experience tremendous success by offering an e-catalog that allows spa enthusiasts across the country to experience the great products used in your spa.

Getting it Made

Take the time to research ad agencies or web design firms that are familiar with the beauty industry. Communicate what you want your image to say and discuss any unique features you may want, like a secure order page that enables gift certificate and product purchases, and a page for gathering information to compile into a database for future mailings.

The average cost for a multi-page site with a secure order page is around $3,000. Expect to spend a minimum of $1,200 for a simple, no bells-and-whistles site, and up to $10,000 for a site with multiple pages, sound, images that fade in and out, etc.

Companies familiar with web development for spas include Prizbie Design at **www.phrizbie-design.com/web_design.html** and Switchfast at **www.switchfast.com/Portfolio_Websites.aspx**. You can also find a wealth of web designers local to you simply by looking in the Yellow Pages under "Computers & Electronics", or "Internet Web Site Design."

Marketing Your Site

One of the first things you'll want to do, even before you build your website, is register your domain name, which is what people will type into the computer to go to your website: www.YourSpaHere.com. For a small monthly fee you can host your site through a service company, register a domain name, and get your site listed on search engines so that clients can find you. One such company is GoDaddy at **www.godaddy.com**.

Be certain all of your printed marketing material contains your web address, and include it on all your press releases. You can also update your website to include clips of media coverage you get.

6.1.2   Direct Mailers

Direct mailers are one of the least expensive methods of advertising, and are a relatively quick and easy way to announce your arrival and promote your spa. Just remember to be consistent with all of your other means of advertising. Saying the same message over and over again and conveying the same image is incredibly important for success.

If you are opening a swanky, high-end spa, stay away from those coupon books that include discounts on furnace cleaning, glass repair, and so on. This is a waste of your money, because you are not targeting the right market.

High-quality postcards work wonderfully as direct mailers. Postage is lower than for an envelope and if designed well, the colors and type-set will grab the attention of everyone who handles it, from the person who sorts the mail at the post office to the mail carrier who delivers it. This is getting more bang for your buck!

You can have a graphic designer put together your postcard, or talk to your local printer about having one designed in-house. Some even offer list-purchasing options (see below) and online design approval to shorten the time from production to mailing. You can also try online companies like Modern Postcard at **www.modernpostcard.com**, which offers postcard design, customized consumer lists, and mailing services.

Who to Send Them to

It's important to have a current, targeted list of potential customers who would be excited about a new spa opening. Just sending direct mailers to everyone in your ZIP code is too general, and doesn't allow for tracking your return on investment.

Purchasing a list from a reputable list broker will give you a much more targeted campaign. You can request (for example) the names and addresses of females under 45 with a household income of $60,000 or more, who travel and frequent spas. You can see how much more valuable that information is than the names and addresses of everyone in a certain ZIP code!

A list broker (found in your local Yellow Pages) will sell you the names and addresses of individuals that fit your target audience. This information is part of databanks that list brokers accumulate through research into buying habits, income levels, etc. It's a great service when the lists are current and relevant, though it can be pricy. If you'd like to get prices and information from list brokers, a couple to contact are Accudata at **www.accudata.com/solution/sales-leads-fast.aspx** and Martin Worldwide at **www.martinworldwide.net**.

Measure Your Success

You can track the success of your mailing by offering something if the customer mentions the postcard when calling to book an appointment.

Say something like "10% off with postcard" so the customer is sure to mention the card, or give a small gift if the customer brings the card in.

Send direct mailers to customers about once every other month to ensure that your business is first in their mind when they consider spa services. Many small business owners stop after sending one mailer. Consistency is the name of the game.

6.1.3   Business Cards

Business cards are often the first image someone gets of your business. In addition to cards for yourself, and possibly your director or manager, you may also want to have some "blank" ones that your staff can write their name on and personalize.

Design Them

Make it count by designing a beautiful, interesting card on good cardstock with simple, easily read fonts. Don't make it too busy, but be sure to include the basics, like your spa's name, address, phone number, and website. Make sure it complements your website, your brochures, your mailers, etc.

Spa business cards can double as appointment reminders if you print a blank line on the back or bottom, under the words "Your Next Visit is..." Many businesses that book appointments do this, since the phone number is literally at the client's fingertips if they need to reschedule.

> **TIP:**   Getting business cards done up for each of your staff is a nice idea, but the spa industry is unfortunately one with a high turnover, so your good intentions could easily be a waste of money.

When you are first launching your spa, you can entice people to come try it out by printing a discount offer (10 or 15% off) on the back of the card. Many businesses do this, and it may work with a spa selling not-too-expensive services.

Think hard about whether price is a concern to your target market, though — when you are selling a "luxury" service, sometimes price is not a motivating factor. Consider whether an offer of free slippers or a gift basket to take home might be more effective in your niche. You should also have a time-limit on using these coupons, since you don't want giving away "free stuff" to cut into your profit once you have an established clientele.

Get Them Out There

In addition to handing out a business card everywhere you meet people, you can be creative in distributing them with some of the following techniques:

- Occasionally leave them behind in places where your target audience is most likely to see them

- Give a stack to your local Chamber of Commerce to include on their business board

- Ask non-competing businesses like bridal shops and health food stores if you can place a small card holder with your cards in their store

- Place them on a community bulletin board

- Supply them to be included in your car dealership's new owner packet (in exchange for free spa services for their manager or their spouse)

- Have them distributed to new moms via the Welcome Wagon or prenatal classes

6.1.4   Brochures

Brochures serve to educate customers about your services and products in a longer format than a business card or a direct mailer.

Usually divided into two or three panels, brochures allow space to convey a significant amount of information. Your brochure can be based on your menu, but printed on high-gloss paper and easier to fold up and carry home.

Finding Marketing Professionals

One spa owner interviewed for this guide had previously worked in marketing with a large advertising firm. When she opened her spa, she chose to put together a team of freelance marketing professionals herself instead of hiring an agency.

"I know personally how ad agencies will focus on the small business owner until a big account, say IBM, comes through the door. I wanted a team of freelancers, and I wanted them to have experience working with small business owners. It has been good for my business and costs a lot less than if I'd gone straight to an agency."

A "team" consists of a public relations professional, a graphic artist for designing your logo, a copywriter for writing your ads, and a website developer. You'll likely pay less and get more individualized service than if you hire someone at a big agency.

Public relations professionals make a living creating media excitement for their clients. They are the alternative to hiring a big-budget advertising agency or marketing firm. They have established relationships with the media and the experience to get your spa noticed by the right sources.

Of course the challenge lies in finding not one, but a team of talented individuals. Many times if you start with your PR professional, they will have freelancers they work with that they can recommend. These professionals should work together to create a seamless identity for your spa.

Websites that feature freelancers looking for paid projects are good starting sources for assembling your marketing team. Try Guru at **www.guru.com** and Mediabistro at **www.mediabistro. com**.

What to Write

Some spas have had success by believing that it's a better idea to teach something in your brochures than simply list services you offer. Highlighting services does not necessarily set you apart from the competition, unless you have a very unique list of services that none of your competitors are offering.

A title like "The Healing Properties of Water Therapy" is a great hook to get your brochure read. Go on to include eight to ten benefits of water therapy (along with research and stats that back up your information), and *then* proceed to inform the reader that all of these benefits are available just three miles from their home in your wonderfully relaxing spa that offers state-of-the-art water therapy facilities.

See how it works? Telling the potential customer something they didn't know before puts you in the position of "expert" in their mind, and helps them to remember your business.

Be sure to include a low-risk way for prospects to take the next step towards purchasing your services. Offer something further that will benefit or educate them. A free seminar or one-on-one consultations are ways to get the potential customer into your spa versus your competitors'.

Even if you are having someone write your brochure, you should still be a big part of the process. It's important that you supply the writer with your logo, your mission statement and any other promotional tools you have already developed. If the writer is local, it's a good idea to have her or him visit your spa to get a feel for the environment.

Guide the writer in the direction of clear, conversational copy that doesn't speak over the head of your prospects. Avoid industry jargon and unfamiliar words. Make sure the writer can draw the reader in by focusing on benefits, not prices.

Getting Help

If you live near a graphics arts school or a university with a strong art department, you might approach a professor about assigning the design of your brochures as an extra-credit project for senior graphic arts or illustration students. Or you can simply put a sign on the student bulletin board and offer a small amount of money if a student would like to take on the project. You'll get creative artwork for free (or almost free), and the student gets a job to include in their portfolio.

Local non-competing businesses are more open to displaying your brochures if they don't represent a hard sell for your business. Show a local doctor how beneficial it is for patients to learn about water therapy or aromatherapy massage, for example, and they'll be happy to tout your business at the reception desk.

6.2 Marketing Techniques

Marketing experts we spoke to say they've seen spa owners allocate amounts as small as 1% of their overall budget to marketing. This represents a lack of understanding about the importance of promoting your spa.

One marketing professional told us, "Spa owners need to understand they aren't as much selling services as they are marketing those services in a way that is appealing to the public. Good marketing gets customers to think of your spa or 'brand' before the other person six blocks away who offers very similar treatments and products."

So what's a healthy amount to allocate to marketing? As much as you can afford, especially in the beginning. Once you are up and running, anywhere from five to ten percent of the total business budget is healthy, and this may be higher depending on your market.

It's not that you can't market a spa without money, and some of the techniques in this section won't cost you a dime, but mixing some money in there is smart business. Here are some of the techniques you can use to market your spa.

A Marketing Plan

As part of your business plan you will develop a marketing plan, which outlines your particular tools and techniques for breaking into the local spa market. Spa director Jeremy McCarthy provides you with this sample marketing outline, which is a point-form version of a complete plan.

Sample Marketing Plan

Objective

- Promote the spa to consumers, customers, travel agents, media

Plan

- Advertising, print material, public relations, direct mail, promotions, and strategic special events

Public Relations

- Press Kit

- Fact Sheet

- General Release

- Key Personnel Profiles

- Menu of Services

- Photography as appropriate

Media Trips

- Invite media to the spa

- Create and operate media trips

- Produce special invitation

- Secure airline and rental car partners for media travel

- Secure confirmations from "A" list media for each trip

- Develop media daily program and itineraries

- Execute program on-site and follow-up with media for story placement

- Secure media gifts

Media Blitz

- October (Downtown and Eastern surrounding towns)
- December (Suburbs and Western surrounding towns)

Photoshoot

- Interiors
- Exteriors
- Signature Treatments

Print Material

- Brochure (4-color mail-out)
- Treatment Menu to coordinate with brochure
- Consumer Direct Mail card or brochure
- Operational collateral (confirmation cards, letterhead)

Strategic Special Events

- Invitations to community for spa party
- Include Spa Cuisine concept into a reception
- Offer sample treatments

Promotions

- Partner with health, wellness and spa publications for sweepstakes trips
- Partner with national radio programs in preferred markets for sweepstakes trips
- Secure promotional opportunities as warranted
- Develop small spa giveaway for promotional use

Direct Mail

- Direct mail piece
- Advertising (local)
- Advertising (local)

6.2.1 Paid Advertising

Paid advertising can produce great results if it is well written and produced with the right customer in mind. Advertising is never cheap, though, so you want to make every dollar count. Bland ads that simply say things like "Grand Opening" or "Best massage in town", or worse, are not even clear on what you are offering, will not get clients through your door.

John Uhrig of Monochrome Marketing Solutions advises that your spa's ads "should make your advantages so obvious that your prospects and customers draw this conclusion: I would have to be an absolute fool to do business with anyone else but you, regardless of price."

When creating ads always ask yourself, what's in it for the consumer? Why should they consider your services and products over anyone else's? Go back to your original brainstorming of ideas, and always keep your spa's mission statement in mind.

The type and amount of advertising you do will depend on your marketing budget and your target audience. You can always start with a small ad and run it frequently — many print publications will offer a discount if you book multiple insertions at once.

What works well for one spa will not necessarily work for others, either. The daily newspaper may have a large readership, but what percentage of that readership are spa goers?

"I ran an ad in the newspaper and it didn't work at all. We find that people refer us to other people who understand what we're doing here and appreciate it. Newspaper ads were just too generalized for what we do," says Terri Malueg-Ray, who runs a niche market spa.

Stefanie Palko, owner of Copperfalls Aveda Day Spa, says, "What works for us are high-end local magazines. We've established a relationship with an advertising agency. We're a high-end spa so our marketing needs to reflect our image. I believe your marketing must represent your level of business."

Most spa owners agree that television is too expensive of a medium to get a good return on the dollar. Also a television commercial has to be produced well or it will cheapen the image of your spa.

Radio is a medium you can use to your advantage. It is more cost-effective than television, but in major metropolitan areas like New York and San Francisco the cost can be between $2,000 to $5,000 for a 30-second spot.

Smaller markets like Harrisburg, Pennsylvania will only cost you $150 for 30 seconds during prime time, including production. Call the radio stations in your area and ask to speak with the sales or manager.

6.2.2   Free Publicity

How do you get the local television and radio station buzzing about your spa, especially if you're in a market heavy with competition? The press is looking for a story angle. They are looking for story ideas that link to current events and help them grab their readers. Here are some great ways to get media attention without spending a dime.

One of the first things you'll do when launching your business is to highlight what makes your spa unique. The owner of Barefoot & Pregnant, a spa just for expectant and new mothers, told us she had no problem getting media coverage because there were no other spas in the area with pregnant women as the focus market. Even national women's magazines printed stories on the unique concept of Barefoot & Pregnant.

Once you are up and running, though, you can no longer call the fact that you are offering your spa services "news" so you'll need to look for a new angle. An effective technique for many is to position yourself as an expert in your field.

If you can write short, informational articles about the benefits of spa treatments, call local magazines and newspapers and ask to get their writer's guidelines. Submit articles that teach something like "How to Make the Most of Your Spa Visit – Six Tips for Your First Spa Experience". Include a short mention at the end about your experience in the spa industry and the name/contact info for your spa.

If you have introduced a new treatment that is not available at the competition, you can also brag about it in a press release (a sample press release is included below). Start with one treatment you offer, and write out a two-page description of it.

How many different angles can you cover? What ingredients does it have, where does it come from, what benefits does it create, who invented it, based on what? After each question ask yourself why. The "why" means, "what benefit does it have for my customer?"

Remember to include the who, what, where, when and why. For press releases to be effective, they have to convey news, not a hard sales pitch. Send the release to radio and newspaper stations. Know what you want to say when they call to follow up. (Don't wing it.)

Sample Press Release

CULTURE SPA EMBRACES MOROCCAN
WEDDING TRADITIONS

Contact: Claire Scotts
(212) 555-1212
For immediate release

September 9, 2008

Rockport, Maine — Quickly becoming the swanky spa of choice for trendsetting brides and their friends, Culture Spa is adding another global experience to their bridal pampering spa: Moroccan Exotic. This latest pre-nuptial package builds on the traditions celebrated in the Northern African region.

With the soft sounds of fusioned Arab-African rhythms and the scents of spiced couscous and mint tea traveling through the air, the bride-to-be and her party will be transported to the streets of Marrakesh without ever stepping foot outside Rockport.

"Our spa's mission is to find new and unique ways to pamper brides, so we turned to the global community for inspiration. We already offer our Indian Bride and Japanese Princess packages," says spa owner Melody Washington.

"Creating an African package opens up a whole new world to our clients, from the traditional finger foods to the famous handcrafted Moroccan rugs on our walls."

The new Africa-themed room has a large bathing pool where a bride can have the traditional hammam (bath) where her bridesmaids help to purify her for her wedding day (more traditional brides can also opt for a private aromatherapy bath instead).

Henna parties are a big part of the celebration the night before Moroccan weddings, so Culture Spa will have a henna artist available to replicate the intricate designs commonly made of ground henna paste.

"Our version is temporary and only lasts about three days. But we've found American brides find the practice fascinating and love the idea of using their body as art on their wedding day," says Washington.

In the last two years Culture Spa's fresh approach to beauty and treatment has been growing in leaps and bounds. They now offer eight different spa packages representing various regions and traditions of the world, including Aussie Bride, French Holiday and Olde England. Spa packages include massage, bath, aromatherapy and makeup application. Prices start at $350.

Full details are available from the spa receptionist at 555-1234, or at their website, **www.culturespaexperience.com**.

6.2.3 Community Involvement

Your involvement in community events will help people to remember your business. Sponsoring events that benefit organizations that fundraise is a great way to help others and promote your business at the same time.

You can volunteer to speak at community events that will reach your target audience. If the local women's organization is having a health fair, volunteer to speak on holistic health, light treatment, or anything interesting that your spa offers that will make a memorable seminar. Send out a press release alerting the media to the seminar.

Also setting up booths at business forums and networking events will get you noticed. Be sure to offer a mini-service like a five-minute shoulder rub or a quick acupressure demonstration to pique interest. Have goody bags on hand with inexpensive trial-sizes of products or gift certificates for services, and promotional materials.

> **TIP:** A potentially huge source of revenue for you is brides-to-be, who often like to have a day of pampering before the wedding to look their best. You can meet and attract them to your spa by attending or sponsoring a prize at local bridal shows.

Whatever your target market, you should be constantly on the lookout for new opportunities to meet future clients. Fitness clubs, yoga classes and bookstores are obvious places where people who are interested in improving their minds and bodies will visit. Think about your target market and where they gather, and become a presence through visits and sponsorship.

Joining community business associations like the Chamber of Commerce establishes you as a committed part of your community and provides networking opportunities. The cost of joining such organizations will vary depending on your geographic area. Call and ask for a membership packet. The U.S. Chamber of Commerce has a member directory at **www.uschamber.com/chambers/directory**.

6.2.4   Market to Groups and Businesses

If your spa is big enough to accommodate groups, capitalize on this to the fullest. You may want to find ways to partner with hotels or conference centers in your community. For groups checking into a hotel, for example, you can have a spa employee at the arrival area with candles burning, soft music playing and aromatherapy diffusing. Give them the message that the spa is a "must-do" activity.

For groups booking meetings you can offer "spa breaks" instead of coffee breaks, with yoga stretches, healthy juices and waters, and perhaps even some mini-massages.

Promoting to groups means getting your information to the people who arrange groups: group coordinators, wedding planners, travel agencies, etc. You will have a spa menu for your services, but it is a good idea to also create some information customized for groups. Remember, their job is to create an incredible program for the group they are coordinating. Anything you can do to make their job easier will help them put people in your spa.

Offering a separate menu of services for groups gives you an opportunity to explain group booking and cancellation polices, as well as a way to suggest different packages and activities that you can offer the group. Group planners have to coordinate a lot of details, so having a list of everything you can do for them might help them plan some classes and activities in your spa without having to look elsewhere.

The spa can even host a spa-themed dinner with healthy cuisine, live soulful music, yoga and tai chi demonstrations, and various stations where guests can sample your spa services. This unique dinner party is an event that guests will not soon forget!

6.2.5   Strategic Partnerships

An excellent way to get referrals is to make informal contacts with individuals who have a connection with wellness and beauty. Also known as strategic partners, these are non-competing but related industries that are likely to be in a position where they can refer their clients to a local spa. Consider who you might connect with in the following markets:

- Personal trainers

- Makeup artists

- Wedding planners

- Image consultants

- Personal shoppers

- Doctors and nurses

- Clothing retailers

- Hair salons

- Plastic surgeons

- Dieticians

- Etiquette trainers

- Dermatologists

- Nail salons

You can contact the manager or owner of these businesses, and ask to come in for a short meeting to discuss how your businesses could benefit each other. You can sweeten the pot by offering them a chance to come by and sample the spa experience free of charge, and see what they think.

At worst they'll probably let you leave a stack of business cards or brochures, and at best, they will become an excellent source of referral business for your spa. In return they can be the business that you refer to your clients.

Some businesses will want a formal agreement or commission, while others will work on a mutual and informal agreement. Select your strategic partners with care, though — you want to make sure that a referral from them is meaningful and is in step with your way of doing business. You don't want your business to suffer because of a bad referral, either.

You can get creative with how you partner with businesses, and it doesn't need to be a long-term agreement. For example, you can package your services with a hotel or chocolate shop and sell them online!

6.3 Creating Client Loyalty

"Client retention rate is the ultimate measure of customer satisfaction. What are you doing to create an experience that is second-to-none and will have clients coming back and spending more money?"

— *Neil Ducoff, Strategies Publishing Group*

Marketing serves to get clients in the door, but once they come, how do you get them to return again and again? The answer is simple: build relationships. In the service industry more than any other field, relationships mean profit.

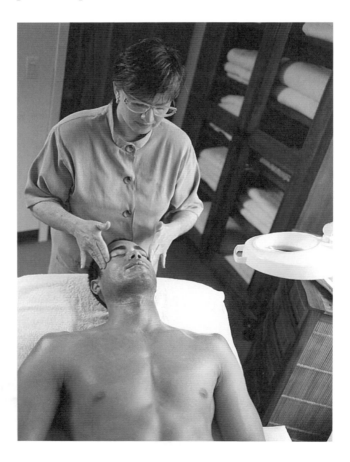

6.3.1   A Personal Touch

Attention to detail is a major way to build client relations, from referring to the client by name when they are in the spa to sending a card on their birthday. We all love to feel special and remembered. Show your clients that they are special to you. Keeping a detailed database will enable you to know the best ways to serve your clients' needs, which translates into more sales and loyalty for your business.

Be as detailed as possible with information under each customer's card. Include their preferences in products, their birthday, anniversary, etc. Use this information to do special things for your customers.

You will have a list of prospects for your database if you chose to use a list broker. And of course, include friends, family, ex-coworkers, local business owners and those who attended your grand opening. You can gather more names and contact information by attending community events and raffling off something related to your spa.

Sample Raffle Entry Card

Name: _____

Date of Birth: _____

Marital Status: *Single / Married / Divorced / Widowed*

Spouse's Name: _____

Wedding Anniversary: _____

Children's Names and Ages: _____

Hobbies and Interests: _____

Most Frequently Used Service: _____

Other Services Used: _____

Services Never Used: _____

Products Purchased: _____

Favorite Staff Member: _____

How Often Do You Visit? _____

Display something eye-catching like a large basket filled with spa products, bathrobe, gift certificate, etc. and then invite those passing by to participate in the raffle. Give them a short informational card to fill out in order to be included. One person will win the wonderful basket of goodies, while you'll have plenty of new names for your direct mail or email campaigns.

> TIP: You should reassure clients that you will not sell or give their personal information to anyone, and give them the option of not being contacted by your spa for special offers and promotions. In these days of telemarketers and junk mail, people are getting leery of trading their names and phone numbers for future harassment.

6.3.2   Reward Word of Mouth

Creating a system that rewards your most loyal customers is to your advantage. Imagine if every customer you serviced raved about your business to several friends! Recommendations are the best advertising you can get. Why not set up your business from the very beginning with a way to say, "I appreciate your business and want you to brag about your experience to your friends."

- To get people talking, create a "brag card". Give out business cards with small codes to each of your regular customers to hand out to their friends. When their friends come to your spa for a service, note the customer who bragged about your spa and send a special gift or offer a discount on services in exchange for a certain number of referrals.

- You can also send out emails or direct mailers to your best customers inviting them to a two-for-one service. If they bring a friend, they both get a service for the cost of one. Be sure to get the friend's contact information and include her or him in your database.

- You can structure a loyalty club for clients who frequent your business often. You can bundle services, offering them one for half price, or give them a sampling of a new service for free.

6.3.3 Ask For Feedback

Spa owners say there's nothing as valuable as customer feedback. It takes the guesswork out of what you're doing. Consider the following ways to keep the channels of communication open and productive.

- Create an e-newsletter that is sent out once a month to customers announcing new treatments, industry trends, color analysis, etc. so your customers look forward to receiving your email every month. Include a request for feedback as part of the content.

- Mail out postcards every two months with small incentives to come in for a treatment, such as an eyebrow wax or free informational seminar on hair coloring. Put a questionnaire on the back to fill in before redeeming the coupon.

- Call customers the day after an appointment and ask them to rate their experience with your spa on a scale of 1 to 5. If the answer is less than 4, ask what could be done to make the service more enjoyable. Be prepared to follow up on suggestions. You could also mail them a short survey instead. (A sample survey appears on the next page.)

- Send out "what would you like to see offered" cards. You can give a checklist of four or five treatments that would be easy to incorporate into your business and let the customers say which one they'd prefer.

Sample Mail Out Questionnaire

[Company Logo – Letterhead]

Name: _____

Address: _____

_____

_____

Phone: _____

Email: _____

Thank you for taking this brief survey. It will help us in our continuing efforts to make Splendid Spas the top day spa in the west. To show our appreciation, bring this survey with you on your next visit and receive a 10% discount on your next treatment.

Please circle the number that best describes your feelings about the service or treatment received at Splendid Spas, where a 1 is unacceptable, and a 5 is absolutely fabulous:

- All spa staff were friendly and met my needs   1 2 3 4 5
- The treatment was what I expected   1 2 3 4 5
- Splendid Spas had everything I was looking for   1 2 3 4 5
- Service providers were helpful and knowledgeable   1 2 3 4 5
- The spa was clean and well organized   1 2 3 4 5
- I left the spa feeling better than when I entered   1 2 3 4 5

To help us meet our clients' needs, please take the time to tell us if there are any treatments or services that you would like to see added:

_____

_____

Thank you for taking the time to fill out this survey.

Sincerely,

J. Smith
Owner, Splendid Spas

6.3.4   Other Ideas from the Experts

"Offer seminars that serve in ways that are not directly linked to your business. One spa I know of offers grief classes for their customers who have suffered loss. They teach healthy ways to grieve and how to take care of oneself physically and emotionally during the process."

"Keep abreast of the developments in your field. New treatments and product ingredients are always being introduced, from LED light treatment to Botox. Even if you don't offer the service, be informed. Customers will ask your opinion and you want to keep your 'expert' status."

"Attend trade shows and read trade publications. Get ongoing training, even in the areas you already know. It never hurts to be exposed to innovative ways of doing what you're already doing."

"A spa I know of displayed a Christmas tree decorated with chocolate fortune cookies. The 'fortune' inside was a gift certificate for a small complimentary service like an eyebrow wax or a nail polish change. The campaign was a successful marketing tool for the spa because customers felt appreciated. Think of creative ways to say 'we appreciate you'."

"Training programs that teach superior customer service skills will help your staff to market your spa consistently with the written material, the logo and the overall image. Help your staff by preparing a blurb about your business, such as 'a fun place for brides to have an international spa experience'. As corny as it may sound, it keeps everyone on the same page and before you know it, even the local community will think of your business exactly the way you want them to."

6.4 Spa Growth Possibilities

No business stays the same forever, and your spa certainly will not. Spa treatments are always evolving and changing, your staff will come and go, you may change suppliers… or you may simply change your mind.

It's important for a healthy business to continue to grow and respond to change. And as your business grows, you may find yourself adding new treatments, staff members and bombarded with business to the point that your current incarnation of a spa is no longer meeting the demands of your clients.

So what's the next step? It starts with examining your possibilities for growth. We've taken a look at three options below, but you can let your ambition take you as far as you choose.

6.4.1   Expanding Your Current Spa

Are you ready to expand your spa with more treatment rooms, more staff, or that relaxation room you overlooked in your initial build-out? The surest sign is in the numbers, as in dollar figures. If you have a healthy profit level and room to grow, why not be able to serve more clients? Signs you are ready for an expansion include:

- A consistently full appointment book for several years

- Losing clients because you can't book them soon enough

- More staff members than you have room for

- A healthy profit

- The capacity to shut down for a while so renovations can take place

If you think that expanding is next on your list of things to do, it's time to go back to the drawing board with your architect and/or spa con-sultant. Take a look at client feedback from the past — what treat-ments are clients asking for that you have been unable to accommodate? Ask your current staff what they would change about the current lay-out or service delivery if they could.

Due to the nature of the spa business, it is unlikely that you will be able to stay open during renovations like a grocery store or mall would. Renovations are notoriously messy, dusty and noisy, and could for-ever destroy someone's image of your spa if their tranquility was ru-ined by any or all of these.

Prepare for your renovations by letting your regular clients know that you will be expanding to serve them better, and get them on board by generating excitement about your new facility. If the renovations will be significant, have your architect prepare a sketch you can show off to clients on an art easel before they take place.

Unfortunately, during the renovations is not your chance to take that long-awaited vacation. Instead, you should be onsite as much as possible, supervising your vision and building a rapport with the contractors to make sure all goes as planned.

When you are ready to reopen, throw the grand opening party you didn't have the cash to put on the first time around. Revamp your menu and website to go along with your new look. Enjoy this time of rebirth and renewal for your business.

6.4.2   Opening More Locations

What if there's no more room to expand where you are at, but your spa is bursting at the seams with clientele, and there seems to be no end in sight? Opening a second location is a big step, but many spa owners have seized this opportunity in the past.

A Similar or "Sister" Spa

In many ways you are back to square one looking for a location, doing a build-out, and hiring again, but you are backed this time by having a strong concept for your spa in place. In the start-up phase the new location is likely to take up a lot of your time and energy, so ensure that you have prepared your staff and systems at the current location to "fly solo" for at bit. Make sure you are still available by cell phone for emergencies.

> **TIP:**   It's even more important in this case to take steps to have all your operational systems in place so that your service is consistent from one location to the next.

If you are opening another location reasonably nearby, the distance away you put the new location is crucial. You want to find a blend of new clients who will come to your spa based on reputation or marketing, and regular clients who are perhaps a bit closer to the new location who will move over and make some room at the old location.

Another possibility lies in opening a location in a new town or city. Don't assume the demographics are exactly the same — you may need to approach the new clientele a bit differently to achieve the same results. If you new location is not too far, you can look to your current pool of employees to move to the new location or possibly manage it. This will help with offering consistent service.

Of course, it's possible that you want to open a new spa that is not a clone of your old one, but a "sister spa" that is unique to its demographics and concept. You can create a buzz about the new location and make the connection by stating this, and by celebrating the grand opening in a smaller way at the old location as well, with special sales and discounts.

Franchising or Licensing

If you are confident that you have a successful business system and want to share it with as many people as possible, "franchising" refers to selling your business system and name to entrepreneurs who want to own a business but don't want to start from scratch (you can review section 3.2.3 on starting a franchise spa for details on and resources for franchises).

Franchising allows you to grow at a faster rate than if you opened several locations on your own. And you still have a tremendous amount of control over how your name, logo and product are presented. Likewise, you can decide exactly what is sold and how things are done when you franchise your name and system.

One aspect of franchising that is particularly appealing is you don't foot the bill for franchises, the franchisee does. You get to build your "brand" with someone else's money. But wait — you have responsibilities to the franchisees as well.

As the franchisor, you are responsible for providing a proven system that someone else can follow to grow their business to the success level that you've grown yours. Marketing and advertising will usually fall on your shoulders, as will training, assistance with business location and sometimes even help with securing finances for operations. The franchisee pays a fee or a percentage of their profits to you for all of these services.

Before you jump on board, note that you are legally liable for problems that occur at franchises. If someone sues a franchisee in California and you're located in Texas, your corporate office will still be called into court. You will also be required by federal law to disclose your financial statements to potential franchisees, as well as personal legal records and information about any criminal record you or your board of directors may have.

If this sounds like something you're ready for, hiring a lawyer who specializes in setting up franchise operations is a good start. The federal and state governments regulate franchises pretty closely. You don't want to get into trouble simply because you didn't do your homework.

A less expensive and less "involved" way of getting your business to the next level is through licensing your business. This can be a tricky area because the lines between a trademark agreement (licensing) and a franchise agreement sometimes blur.

Very generally speaking, a licensing agreement gives you less control over what is done with your trademark and business image. And you can't collect franchise fees since you aren't actually a franchise.

Most entrepreneurs who purchase licensing agreements believe they already know how to run a business sufficiently, but want to get into a market with a recognizable brand instead of building brand awareness. With licensing, you aren't legally liable for mistakes made by licensees; however, that doesn't mean their problems can't damage your business image.

Most franchises start out as licensing agreements because there's less paperwork and cost involved. However, it's smart to still use a lawyer to help with the fine details.

6.4.3   Opening a Resort Spa

If you live in a particularly beautiful or touristy destination, one avenue for growth lies in making your day spa into a "stay spa". Your guests would have all their needs met while staying at your spa for a length of time, including food and overnight accommodations.

Begin by looking at your current spa location. Can it be renovated into a place of accommodation and dining? If not, you will you need to move your spa services to a new location that can have sleeping quarters and a dining area as part of the facility. A nice match for a smaller resort/day spa is a current bed and breakfast, which will already have structures and amenities in place for guests to stay.

To draw clients to your resort spa, you will want to plan to treat your guests to special events, fitness classes, or lifestyle training sessions that are in keeping with your spa's theme. You would hire a director of programs to coordinate your guests' visits.

Facilities you could consider adding to basic accommodations include:

- Swimming pool

- Hot tub/sauna

- Outdoor gardens

- Fitness room

- Entertainment lounge

The cost to build this type of facility is high, but there are investors out there who would love to get involved with a spa of this type — perhaps even your current spa clients!

If you think it's possible to take your spa in this direction, work out the details, get a business plan, and shop it around. You'll have the business skills and experience of running your own spa to draw on, and for many investors, this is the surest sign of a sound investment.

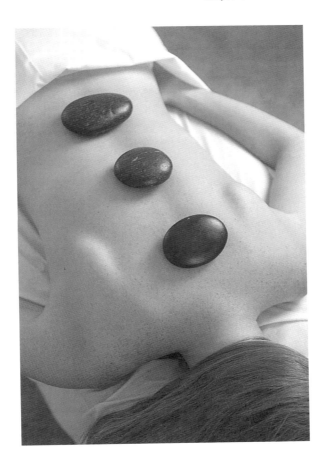

7. Conclusion

Opening your own spa can be one of the most exciting and creative ventures of a lifetime. What you are creating has the power to positively affect the life of another human being within a few short hours. A spa sanctuary allows you the opportunity to give others the gifts of serenity, healing, insight and joy.

You have reached the end of the *FabJob Guide to Become a Spa Owner*, but hopefully this is also the beginning of your journey to successful spa ownership. You can use the resources listed below to delve even deeper into the myriad of information that is out there about spas and the spa life. As you develop your spa, enjoy the journey as well as the thrill of reaching the destination. Good luck!

Spa Owner Resources

Equipment Suppliers

- *Beauty Design*
  www.beautydesign.com

- *Belvedere Co.*
  www.belvedereco.com

- *CCI Beauty*
  www.ccibeauty.com

- *J'Vita Spa Line*
  www.spaline.ca

- *Spa Elegance*
  www.spaelegance.com

- *Spa Manufacturers, Inc.*
  www.spamanufacturers.com/swim_spa.php

- *Takara Belmont*
  www.takarabelmont.com/ourproducts/catalog.php

Miscellaneous Suppliers

- *At Peace Media*
  www.atpeacemedia.com

- *Bath Accessories Company Inc.*
  www.bathaccessories.com

- *Chadsworth and Haig*
  www.chadsworthandhaig.com

- *Cypress*
  www.cypressbathrobes.com/wholesale

- *Hay House*
  www.hayhouse.com

- *JMT Beauty*
  http://jmtbeauty.com/main.htm

- *Milk and Honey*
  www.milkandhoneyinc.com

- *Pendergrass Inc.*
  www.pendergrassinc.com

- *Robe Works*
  www.robeworks.com

Uniforms

- *PureGiving*
  www.puregiving.com/smocks.htm

- *Salon Wear*
  www.salonwear.com

- *Spa Uniforms Inc.*
  www.spauniforms.com

Spa Retail Products

- *Deserving Thyme*
  www.deservingthyme.com

- *June Jacobs*
  www.junejacobs.com

- *Naturopathica*
  www.naturopathica.com

- *Sundari*
  www.sundari.com

- *Via Botanica Body Care*
  www.botanicabodycare.com

Spa Private Label Products

- *Aromatherapy Associates*
  www.aromatherapyassociates.com

- *Spa Factory Bali*
  www.spafactorybali.com

- *The Goddess Ltd.*
  www.aromatherapywholesale.com

- *Unique Candles*
  www.uniquecandles.net

Spa Treatment Products

- *Creative Spa*
  www.creativenaildesign.com

- *J'Vita Spa Line*
  www.spaline.ca/Catalogue.html

- *Kerstin Florian*
  www.kerstinflorian.com

- *Pevonia Botanica*
  www.pevonia.com

- *Sothys Paris*
  www.sothys-usa.com

Spa Software

- *Elite Software*
  www.elitesoftware.com

- *ProSolutions Spa Salon and Resort Software*
  www.prosolutionssoftware.com/index.asp

- *Salon Iris*
  www.saloniris.com/clienttracking.htm

- *SpaBiz*
  www.spabiz.com

- *SpaSoft*
  www.springermiller.com/spasoft

- *SpaWorks*
  www.spaworks.com

Spa Magazines

- *American Spa*
  www.americanspamag.com/americanspa

- *Day Spa*
  www.dayspamagazine.com

- *Massage Magazine*
  www.massagemag.com/Magazine

- *Skin Inc.*
  www.skininc.com

- *Spa*
  www.spamagazine.com

- *Spa Asia*
  www.spaasia.com

- *Spa Management Journal*
  www.spamanagement.com

Online Resources

- *About.com Spas*
  www.spas.about.com

- *Spa Central*
  www.spa-central.com

- *Spa Finder*
  www.spafinder.com

- *Spa Look*
  www.spalook.com

- *Spa Trade*
  www.spatrade.com

- *The Salon Channel*
  www.salonchannel.com

- *Virtual Spa*
  www.virtualspa.com

Save 50% on Your Next Purchase

Would you like to save money on your next FabJob guide purchase? Please contact us at **www.FabJob.com/feedback.asp** to tell us how this guide has helped prepare you for your dream career. If we publish your comments on our website or in our promotional materials, we will send you a gift certificate for 50% off your next purchase of a FabJob guide.

Get Free Career Advice

Get valuable career advice for free by subscribing to the FabJob newsletter. You'll receive insightful tips on: how to break into the job of your dreams or start the business of your dreams, how to avoid career mistakes, and how to increase your on-the-job success. You'll also receive discounts on FabJob guides, and be the first to know about upcoming titles. Subscribe to the FabJob newsletter at **www.FabJob.com/newsletter.asp**.

Does Someone You Love Deserve a Dream Career?

Giving a FabJob® guide is a fabulous way to show someone you believe in them and support their dreams. Help them break into the career of their dreams with more than 75 career guides to choose from.

Visit www.FabJob.com to order guides today!

More Fabulous Books

Find out how to break into the "fab" job of your dreams with FabJob career guides. Each 2-in-1 set includes a print book and CD-ROM.

Get Paid to Help People Look Fabulous

Discover how to get paid to show people and companies how to make a fabulous impression. The **FabJob Guide to Become an Image Consultant** shows you how to:

- Do image consultations and advise people about: total image makeovers, communication skills, wardrobe, and corporate image

- Start an image consulting business, price your services, and find clients

- Select strategic partners such as makeup artists, hair stylists, and cosmetic surgeons

- Have the polished look and personal style of a professional image consultant

Get Paid to Apply Makeup

Learn how to apply makeup to your spa clients or discover how to get hired as a professional makeup artist. In the **FabJob Guide to Become a Makeup Artist** you will discover:

- How to apply makeup like a professional makeup artist to best suit someone's coloring, skin type, face, shape and features

- How to choose a makeup artist training program

- How to get a job as a makeup artist for a salon, spa, retail store, or cosmetics company

- How to get freelance work as a makeup artist for advertisements, magazines, movies, music videos, runway shows, television, and theater

Visit www.FabJob.com to order guides today!